KNICKERBOCKER GLORY

An Orphan's Story

by J.C.G. Lowdell

Harmony Book – HB/01

Printed & Published by Amazon KDP
1st Edition (Re-Proof)

Designed with larger fonts to make it easier to read for those with sight impairments. ***glaucomarize.org***

ISBN: 9798398816662

CONTENTS

PREFACE

This book has taken me a year to write, and many years beforehand thinking about it!
I was first inspired to write my story when, after an online search, I realized little was being written about our history and the times when I was growing up in care in the 1970's.
It felt to me that somehow our legacy was being forgotten.
Then a dedicated new team from Spurgeon's Childcare began a mission to preserve and celebrate the lives and memories of the children whom they had previously looked after, and I was asked and encouraged to write my childhood memoir.
All about my growing up, half of my childhood in care, and the incredible times we came from, and lived through.
Especially, as the new philosophies of this age have sought to criticise and undermine our culture, traditions, values and beliefs; and even the very times we came from.
So this book is written with inspiration, passion and defiance, and with a true and open heart. It's also my sincere hope that it has captured the spirit and memories of those times.

It's also written with a genuine desire to reach out to my brethren who also came from broken homes - those who have been in orphanages, children's homes or foster care.
We are all children of circumstance, all of us with a story, all of us with trauma and scary memories, in one form or another.

But this is a story of survival and faith. And my prayer is that it will inspire others to try to stay positive and brave in the face of adversity and life's challenges and tragedies. I realize that every single one of us will have experienced events differently, and so in essence, we all have our own versions and our own feelings about what happened to us.

Indeed, I have siblings who went through the same care system; but I can only tell it from my own point of view. At every juncture, I have tried to be fair, as impartial as possible, and to think of everyone in a positive light, regardless of whether I got on well with them, or not. Although to be fair, I have always got on well with the majority of folks! I have not tried to disguise names - I have simply used everyone's real first names, whilst predominantly using initials for surnames.
Nor have I tried to provoke or upset people, nor do I bear any grudges against anyone. So if there is any person who is unhappy with anything I've said in this narrative - well I'm sorry - I'm just not the kinda guy who deliberately sets out to hurt people; so if anyone takes umbrage well, you'll just have to sue me! 💪 I answer to a higher authority anyway!
I am also grateful for my life and my childhood, for better or for worse, and always see life as one's own personal movie. And any great movie is filled with joy and sorrow, happiness and tragedy, mystery, irony and humour. And I believe that my own amazing life movie is definitely worthy of a book. So here we are - peeling back the layers of my life through the sands of time and the fields of experience.
It's also my own personal story and in the end, not only the tale of a most challenging childhood, but also a story of survival, desire, love and serendipity. ☯

J.C.G. Lowdell
June 2023

"Adapt – Improvise – Overcome"
Bear Grylls

DEDICATION

In loving memory of my parents

Wendy Mary & Geoffrey D.S.P Lowdell

Who Gave Me Life

LOWDELL COAT OF ARMS

"Nemini Obesse Sed Omnibus Prodesse"

To be a burden to no one, but to benefit all

EPIGRAPHS

I've done all I can, now it's out of my hands, stand on my head
and say ... oh, I was just a boy ... giving it all away...
Sail away, sail away...
Ooh, I know better now, I know better now ...
Giving it all away. Just a boy ... giving it all away.
I was just a boy...

Leo Sayer / David Courtney - "Giving it all Away" by Roger Daltrey © 1973

I was born in white on a hot summer night,
With the moon glow NEW with a powerful pull,
Everybody dreamed and everyone knew 'twas savage.
Little boy lost in a childhood frost,
But he grew real keen and he grew real mean,
Everybody dreams and everyone knows it's savage.
Fire inside like a burning bride,
Where the tide subsides and the leopard cub hides,
Everybody dreams but everyone knows it's wild.
Pounding on my brain like a runaway train,
Are the voices of the people that I left in the rain,
But everybody dreams and everyone knows it's savage.
Born to be real, be a prince of the feel,
To be hot on the heel of your own big wheel,
Everybody feels and everyone knows it's savage.

Jayl - "Four Beasts in One" © 2002

When I was a child, I talked like a child, I thought like a child, I reasoned like a child. When I became a man, I put the ways of childhood behind me. For now we see only a reflection as in a mirror; then we shall see face to face. Now I know in part; then I shall know fully, even as I am fully known.
And now these three remain: faith, hope and love. But the greatest of these is love.

1 Corinthians 13:12-13

INTRO – Summer 73 – Dreamland - *by Jayl*

“Ever been to **Dreamland** John?” asked Dougie S, sitting under a Dymchurch willow tree on a glorious August big sky day, in the long hot summer of ‘73. Instantly, for a highly enthusiastic and passionate young boy of 11 years old, the name “Dreamland” in itself conjured up joy and excitement of potentially mythical status. “Noooo” says John, “Where is thaaaat?”

“A place called Margate” answered his friend. “And it’s the greatest funfair in the whole of England!” “Wow!” exclaims John. “What’s the ghost train like?” John’s first excited question. “Much bigger than ours in Dymchurch” says Dougie. “Actually the scariest and longest ghost train in the whole world!” (the world at that time didn’t extend much beyond the local area of Romney Marsh). Dougie then proceeded to describe in great detail a massive and special place of pure enchantment, magic and fun. Wide eyed little John was sold. **In his dreams he dreamed of Dreamland.** He imagined riding the ghost train and the most wild and crazy rollercoasters. The rock n’ roll music and the dodgems, the scenic railway and the magnificent big wheel. The buzz, bells and tunes from fruit machines of every conceivable kind and especially his wild wizardry favourites – a massive selection of the best Bally pinball machines on the planet.

Most of all, little John thought it must be a place filled with endless laughter and fun, and especially pretty girls in pretty clothes and smiling happy people. In his heart he knew that he would go there one day. When that might be, he could not know (and time moves differently for a child); but even at this early stage, his heart spoke words of truth to him. John was a very bright and perceptive boy.

Approaching Dreamland – Margate Sea Front – 1970's

"Just let me hear some of that 'Rock 'n Roll music
Any old way you choose it!
It's got a back-beat, you can't lose it –
Any old time you use it.
It's gotta be rock and roll music
If you wanna dance with me!"

Chuck Berry

PRELUDE – Autumn 74 – Spurgeons - *by Jayl*

One year on, it came to pass that he found himself arriving at Spurgeons Homes for Children – Birchington (near Margate) one cool crisp autumnal day.

It was October 30th 1974 – Halloween Eve. *This is the night that Muhammad Ali became heavyweight champion of the world for the second time when he knocked out George Foreman in the "Rumble in the Jungle." Jamaican Singer Ken Boothe had just hit No.1 in the charts with his smooth classic "Everything I Own". And Arsenal were joint bottom of the First Division after 14 games! Crazy times!* But how had he arrived at this place? What sort of dramatic twist of fate had transpired to send him here? What did this uncertain future now hold? What strange and remarkable destiny might be at hand?

Here, we must allow John to tell his own story….

1962 – 1970 – Children's Paradise

I was born in Folkestone on the lovely summer evening of Aug 2nd 1962, just after the Leo New Moon. Like our late great Queen Elizabeth, my parents were children of the 1920's – the generation that grew up during World War 2. They were wonderful people, but also forthright and strict, with 'old school' principles and ideas. We went to church on Sunday and grew up with all the ancient Christian traditions and values. But my early childhood was a happy one. I had 4 lovely big half-sisters (from my Mother's first marriage) who helped look after me and doted on me; and then later a little sister and 2 little brothers. We lived in a detached house called 'Runnymede' at High Knocke in Dymchurch, on the beautiful and historic Romney Marsh – also known as the 'Children's Paradise'.

Runnymede, High Knocke, Dymchurch - 1960

We could see the sea and were 5 minutes from the most glorious beach. We would be awakened by the Dungeness foghorn on a summer's morn and know that a glorious sunny day awaited us. We also had a wonderful garden to play in. There was very little money, but my parents were adept at managing their household and large family on the resources available and adapting and improvising. Mummy had actually been due a substantial inheritance, coming from such an illustrious background; but alas, after a major fall-out with her Father – Grandpa Denis, and converting from Catholicism to the Church of England, she was disinherited. From then on, life was a lot tougher, but my parents and our family made do. And overall, I can say I felt warmth and loved. My Dad would grow all our own vegetables and fruits, so throughout the year, there would be resplendent harvests for the family to gather in. He worked very hard as a school groundsman at an Ashford Girl's Grammar School (*from the generation who never took a day off*), and he would do all the maintenance on the house himself. At times he could be charming and engaging, but he could also be a rather stern and scary disciplinarian. But he did love us, even though he didn't always show it. *The war generation often seemed less demonstrative.* Of one thing I am certain, he always tried to do what he

believed to be the best for his family. There were huge bonfires with fireworks on November 5th and happy, fun-filled and joyous family Christmases and parties. And we were growing up on the famous Romney Marsh, (aka the Children's Paradise), and

for me it was just that. The amazing historic steam trains of the Romney, Hythe and Dymchurch Railway going right past our garden. **A railway I have loved and been a member of all my life.* The funfair and amusement arcades. The beautiful scenery and wildlife. Endless secret and historic places - castles, forts, pillboxes, towers and ancient iconic churches. Myths and legends, tunnels and smugglers. And the glowing haze of long summer days; of fetes and festivals, music and dance. Sweet shops and fish n' chips (a treat then). Blackberry picking in late summer and shrimping on the beach. And oh what a beach! A vast sandy expanse of lovely golden sand, where the

Dymchurch Beach © Alex Brunsdon

tide seems to go out for miles and then races in swiftly across Dymchurch Bay, swallowing the sand castles and then right up to the huge wall that protects the land, below sea level; reclaimed from the ocean over the centuries. And on full and new moons, the tidal swells and surges could be huge. There would also be mighty and ferocious channel storms. But in summer, under those

Huge Tides – Dymchurch Wall

famous big blue skies and a fat smiling sun, the beach was the place to be. Sun, sand and sea. With days that seemed to last forever! ☼

Dymchurch Wall – Looking West

Yes, my dear Mother (*I only ever knew as Mummy*), had chosen well in where to locate her family; the perfect place for herself and her new man and 4 girls. And after a miserable first marriage, she met my Father – Geoffrey, who essentially rescued her. She divorced her first husband, and married him in October 1960. They had actually been advised that it might be difficult for her

Mum and Dad - 1960

to have more children. Nevertheless, this did not deter him, as he was devoted to her and they loved each other. So they set up home together and when I arrived, I really was a most special miracle baby. And being born in the Children's Paradise in the height of summer – well how blessed was I? My first winter however (*the infamous 'Big Freeze' of early 63*), was most challenging for my parents to keep me warm enough. *No central heating in those days!* But eventually spring returned, followed soon by my first full summer. And how I loved it! 😊

Proud Parents & Sister Rosie - Dymchurch Beach Summer 63

Proud Mum & Sisters
Dymchurch Beach
Summer 63

And then I experienced the joy of having 3 younger siblings (Bill, Elizabeth and Edward); each born 2 years apart. And from the moment they were born, I was extremely protective over all of them.

Protective of my Brother Bill - 1965

My Father was more of a practical man, than an intellectual or musical, but he was the grandson of one Frank Muspratt – professor of music and organist at Limerick Cathedral for 25 years. And his Father (my Grandpa George), was a very fine singer and a member of the world-renowned Canterbury Cathedral Choir. Dad's Mother (Grandma Eileen), was from Limerick in Ireland. She came over to England and got a degree at Cambridge, during the time of suffrage, when this was a rare achievement for a woman.

She later ran her own school in Brighton where my Dad was born. Her and her Sister (my Great Aunt Gladys), were also 2 of the founding members of the Cat's Protection League. So the love of cats is very much in my genes. 🐈

Mummy experienced a difficult childhood during the war, where she grew up with two elderly aunts in Golders Green. Her Mother (Grandma Christine Parkes), had died when she was only 1 year old, during childbirth. Tragically, the baby, who would have been Mummy's little sister, also died. Mummy was the granddaughter of one Adelina de Lara - descended from Spanish nobility; a world-famous concert pianist and protégé of Clara Schumann. So there were

powerful and prominent musical genes surging through my veins from the very start. 🎼 Adelina's son (Grandpa Denis Shipwright), was a controversial and colourful character – a Brooklands racing driver,

squadron leader in World War II and at one time, Conservative MP for St.Ives. *He also had 3 other children (Mummy's half-sisters and brother - Edward), but we never knew about them until years later.* ☹
There was no way of telling that time was desperately short, but Mummy recognized that she had an extremely talented, bright, inquisitive, precocious and highly sensitive little boy, who asked "Why, where and how?" to almost everything! And indeed she did teach me 'everything'. Not literally of course, but everything I would need to fare well at school and later in tougher circumstances. Most of all the morals, ideals and principles I would need to survive and thrive in life. The ethics, standards and education passed down to her, that had made her so strong in mind, body and spirit; she tried to instil in to all of us. She taught me impeccable manners, etiquette and chivalry.
She taught me to be kind and to do unto others as I would expect done to me. She taught me values of community, fairness, tolerance.
The Ten Commandments (*which always made sense*) and The Lord's Prayer (*also made sense*). 🙏 She taught me to always do my best and never give up. She instilled in to me courage and to be focussed and strong in my attitude. To listen to wise counsel and always be willing to learn. She taught me about our most special and dutiful Queen, and to be a patriot. And to sing the hymns with gusto! And like my Father, she gave me a love of nature and trees and animals.

I particularly loved cats and she nurtured this in me too. We had a lovely black boy, Blackie. And later, a ginge called Mij.

Loved cats from the very start. Aged 1 - playing with Blackie 🐈

"The Owl and the Pussy-cat went to sea
In a beautiful pea-green boat,
They took some honey, and plenty of money,
Wrapped up in a five-pound note.
The Owl looked up to the stars above,
And sang to a small guitar,
"O lovely Pussy! O Pussy, my love,
What a beautiful Pussy you are,
You are, You are! What a beautiful Pussy you are!"

Edward Lear

Dymchurch Beach – 1964

Grandma's deadly walking stick!
Dymchurch Beach - 1965

Dymchurch Beach – 1966

Dad passing on his 'green fingers' to me - 1966

Dymchurch Fete Fancy Dress 1969 - The Jack of Hearts + Wee Willie Winkle & Liz Bo Peep

First 'Girlfriend' 1967 ☺

With Bill & Lizzie

With Rosie & Bill

'I am the sea' – Aged 5

Mij & Blackie - 1970

Fun on Beach 1968

Mummy taught me to read and write and play chess before I even went to primary school and I was an avid reader with a thirst for knowledge; taking it all in. Later she taught me cooking and gardening (the latter also inspired by my 'green-fingered' Dad). She also taught me how to treat the girls with respect; to always open the door for a lady and don my cap too! She nurtured my talent for creative writing and history. She tuned me in to football – she must have known! ⚽
She encouraged me to believe in myself and despite being rather high-functioning, intense and passionate, I grew in to a confident, intelligent and popular little boy. I was also very fortunate to attend the best primary school there ever was – Dymchurch Primary – where I met so many great friends - girls and boys; many of whom are now lifelong friends. It was a special class of amazing lovely children who also grew in to amazing lovely adults.
The learning was extensive, with values and ideals passed down over centuries. My thirst to learn and absorb knowledge were boundless and I always strove to be at the top of the class! All the great British 🇬🇧 celebrations and traditions were nurtured and encouraged by the school and parents alike. We learned the national anthem and to respect our country and local community. Boys were boys and girls were girls. There was innocence and clarity. Myself and my friends would play together all over the Marsh and the beaches.

The picture above is of Miss Whitlock's class – Dymchurch Primary 1972. It's such a blessing that I actually remain, to this day, friends with many of the children in this shot, and some from the opposite class too, (not in this shot). Such a special group of people. First friends – lasting friends. I consider them like family and they treat me like family.

We would attend each other's wonderful birthday parties throughout the year and most importantly – despite the inevitable occasional childhood spat, we were always kind and tolerant with one another, slow to anger and quick to forgive; and without spite or gaslighting. We were also blessed with one of the greatest periods of musical history there has ever been – the glorious late 60's and early 70's. There were just so many inspirations, and very early my sister Wendy tuned me in to The Beatles and then Top of the Pops. Life would never be the same again! 🤩

Dymchurch Primary Official Photo
@ the Sacred Bridge, behind the school. Aged 8

Dr.Meredith – Vicar of Dymchurch
Day of Syn 64

And in Dymchurch we would have the annual Day of Syn (celebrating the famous character), with historical and joyful pageants and old-fashioned village fetes. There were village treasure hunts and fancy-dress competitions. And a re-enactment on the beach of a contraband landing by the Scarecrow (alias Dr.Syn and normally played by the Vicar of Dymchurch), and his band of smugglers and night riders. Fairground and ghost train in full swing, the enticing aromas of fish 'n chips and candy floss; and also the regular iconic, varied and sonorous whistles of the steam trains of the RHDR. 🚂

'The Scarecrow' Lands - Dymchurch Beach
Day of Syn 64

We learned which whistle belonged to which engine. *And with a lifetime association with this railway, something I can still do to this day!*😊*#SteamTherapy*

No.1 Green Goddess – Hythe Station - 1960's

As I was only a little boy, I of course looked at life with 'rose-tinted specs'; but throughout 1969 there were signs and portends of trouble on the horizon, both in the wider world and in my own self-contained smaller world. The troubles in Northern Ireland were growing worse, and the Vietnam War too. And my dear and educated Grandma Eileen had become extremely unwell, as her dementia became severe. And in the Spring of 69 she was committed to Chartham Hospital – an old Victorian mental asylum, whose very name used to fill people with trepidation and fear.

**In writing this memoir, I have read a lot of diaries. These included Mummy's, Dad's, Great Aunt Gladys and Grandma's. The last diary for Grandma is from 1968, and it was deeply saddening to witness for myself her confusion and pain. There are entries that refer to how muddled she felt in her mind. And reading her sister Glady's account of her descent in to madness, was particularly harrowing. The saddest part of all was my Grandma being separated from her beloved cats, which absolutely broke her, and there is nothing quite so real and raw as a personal diary.*

Mummy's description of events relates to her and Dad's practical worries and concerns about Grandma, and of course Grandpa George – who must have been going through a most awful time himself.

And also Mummy had her own serious health problems. In February 1969, she awoke with a terrible bleeding from the nose and it couldn't be stopped.

So much so, she actually nearly died then. Not that I knew that, but I do remember the shock and panic of the bleeding and Mummy being taken to hospital. She did have clotting issues with her blood, which alas, would eventually and tragically present themselves again. Furthermore, having 8 healthy children had taken its toll on her and she had women's problems, particularly concerning her womb, with an op booked for the following year.

At the start of November 69 there were floods on the Romney Marsh after a prolonged period of severe rain and by the end of the month there were snows. And after his difficult year, Grandpa moved in with us. But he was very unwell and not his usual jolly self at all.

**In his later years Grandpa was an actor for the BBC with bit parts on BBC shows like "Oh Father" with Derek Nimmo. He also had a small part in "The Saint" with Roger Moore. And was Father Christmas on the popular children's show "Crackerjack" (5-to-5 on a Friday), which was wonderful fun!* This is how I most remember Grandpa – with his big rosy cheeks, making us laugh and telling stories of his acting adventures in London. But in this particular year of 1969, he was understandably, a shadow of himself.

Grandpa George in The Saint - 1965

Mummy's diary entries for 1969 and early 1970, although she only wrote short notes, demonstrate the sheer volume of concerns and anxieties she was facing; with many of her entries being worries about the health and well-being of us – her children. In those days, before more modern medicines and care, there was always one of us 'coming down' with some 'bug' or other; and invariably, if one of us got it, we all got it! So constant trips to Dr.Simpson, or he visiting the house.**In those days, one's Doctor tended to be a family friend, or at least someone who knew all the family and would know all his patients personally.*
In that December, my half-sister Lissa left school early to help Mummy look after us all. Alas, poor Mummy had also slipped and broken her leg a year or so before, so this must have been very challenging.
But that year of 1969, we also had a rare and magical white Christmas; and as a child oblivious at this stage to life's true brutality, I distinctly recall a deep feeling of happiness. I still remember that Christmas Eve – beautiful serene snowfall. I stood on our doorstep with Mummy talking to a neighbour feeling so happy, strong and proud to be her son and I would fight for her (or my siblings) always. I was already growing up to be a fiercely loyal and protective kinda guy. But I learned. Some things you can't protect against. Who could have predicted that glorious Christmas would be her last with us?

Summer 1970 – Tragedy

In 1970 the Beatles disbanded (massive news at the time) and the legendary Jimi Hendrix died. And this coincided with a tragedy so dreadful and traumatic that it essentially ripped the heart out of our family. On a beautiful summer's day, 4 days before my 8th birthday, Mummy went in to hospital for a hysterectomy operation (routine op these days). Alas, something went terribly wrong and she essentially bled to death. Who or what was at fault remains a mystery to this day, but the matriarch and force who held our family together was gone. I felt like she had been personally taken from me by God himself and I just didn't get why he would have done this to me. I felt abandoned and lost. 😢

But my lessons ran deep, and even then, I trusted that the Almighty had a higher purpose, so I remained faithful. But doubts had crept in to my soul and I did start to become very troubled – symbolized by nightmares, bed-wetting and occasional distressing tantrums that I found hard to control. Nevertheless, Mummy had taught me "Que sera sera – what will be, will be", so I got on with life with the eternal optimism and positivity I've always naturally possessed. 💪

My half-sister Lissa (who was close with my Dad), bravely stepped up to look after him and us. And in such challenging circumstances (and coping with her own crushing grief), she kept the household and family

going for 4 years. My other half-sisters would also 'muck in' and help in so many ways; and so despite our devastating loss, the family kept going.
And personally, I continued to flourish at school and enjoy life. How could I not, with such wonderful and caring friends, who treated me no differently? Certainly not like a victim. And one of my best friends – Philip M, also lost his Mum at the same age as me, so I was not alone. And those first years of the 70's were an exciting period for kids growing up; a time that included momentous events as well as sweeping cultural and artistic changes in both the country and the world.

The 8 of us (taken by my Dad)– August 1970 – And placed in Mummy's grave

*"It's the freakiest show. Take a look at the Lawman
Beating up the wrong guy, Oh man! Wonder if he'll ever know
He's in the best-selling show - Is there Life on Mars?"*

David Bowie

Early 70's and The Arsenal - 1970 – 1974

Most prominent in my memory of this period – black and white news featuring the IRA and the Northern Ireland troubles; and the same old traditional fray between the Tories and Labour – in this time it was Wilson v Heath (Tory leader and PM from Thanet who took on the miner's union, and lost).
So I clearly remember power cuts, decimalization, and joining the Common Market and when it was just BBC 1, 2 or ITV. The wrestling on cold winter Saturday afternoons, before the iconic classified results (with pools coupons), followed by Dr.Who – at that time played by the great Jon Pertwee. We played a lot of board games, like Monopoly, Cluedo and my favourite, the horse racing game – Totopoly. And a myriad of playing card games. We watched comedy classics like "Fawlty Towers", "Dad's Army", and "Are you being served". The great war movies – "The Battle of Britain" and "633 Squadron". And this was the time of glitter and glam. David Bowie, Elton John, Wizzard, Slade, The Sweet, the ELO and T.Rex. And after I heard "Life on Mars" (which changed my world), I began the Dymchurch Primary School lunchtime 'Top of the Pops', where everyone was encouraged to write songs, sing, play glockenspiels or just bang a drum! 🥁 It was when I wrote my first songs. The very first one called "I wanna go home"; I just sang my own words to the tune of the Beach Boys "Sloop John B!" But the second one,

"Never see you again" (perhaps written with my Mum in mind), I actually made up my own first simple tune. ♫ I would also write stories (normally in the ghostly / monster category), and would read them to the class. Even at such a young age, I was an instigator, knew my own mind and wasn't afraid to express myself. Our little school had 2 football teams – the A Team, who got to play against other schools, and the B Team (essentially the A team reserves). But those of us not necessarily blessed with the most natural footballing skills (or just late developers), were mainly just left on the sidelines, without any coaching or proper game time at all. So I went to the headmaster, asked him if I could form a C Team, and he agreed. So I put together the team, we challenged the B Team to a match, and beat them 4-3! This is the attitude of defiance that has always been at the very core of my character. And after all, music and football were my first loves. And it was during this time I made the vital decision that every young boy (or girl) has to make; which football team to choose as a lifetime allegiance. *For once chosen – tis' in the blood.* My favourite footballer was Alan Ball, who played for Everton and England when I first showed an interest, after Mummy had introduced me to the sport. But it was the 1971 Cup Final, and a wonderful London team wearing vibrant yellow & blue, and that iconic winning goal beating Liverpool 2-1 in extra time – by the one and only Charlie George, that made the decision easy for me. It was to be Arsenal. 👍

Of course! 😉 One of the great decisions of my life; and even better, given that Alan Ball soon became an Arsenal player and actually captain.

Alan Ball – Captain of Arsenal – Highbury 1973 + Charlie George with the FA Cup – May 1971 © Getty Images

Meanwhile, I continued to enjoy my life in Dymchurch – at school and with my friends; growing, roaming, studying the history, and loving our Children's Paradise. The Romney Marsh; full of alcoves, history, mysteries; and legends like the famous parson/ smuggler – Doctor Syn; *depicted in Russell Thorndike's novels – read many times.*

Alas, in December 1971, I had my first experience of animal loss, with the death of our beloved family cat – Blackie. This was actually the first time I'd ever seen my Dad cry, when he informed me that he'd just buried him in the garden. 😢

In July 1972, Grandma passed away at home, aged 75. I was not informed of this event; or if I was, I don't recall being overly affected. Perhaps I'd just got used to her not being around anyway. My Dad must have had terribly mixed feelings, although he wasn't one for always showing his emotions. The pain and sadness of an only son losing his dear mother, who once doted on him, against the relief of not having to watch her suffer any more from such a tragic and dibilitating dementia. Perhaps I wasn't told all about Grandma to save me any further pain or confusion.

I realize now that at times I was traumatized by Mummy's passing; my horrible bed-wetting was one manifestation of this, as well as on occasion - terrible nightmares. Nevertheless, I tried to make the best of everything and mostly had a sunny and optimistic disposition. And my sister Lissa was a fabulous cook (just like Mummy), and my Dad continued to grow his delicious fruit and veg and we still went blackberry picking. Romney Marsh blackberries - most juicy and succulent in the country.

Blackberry picking with my siblings - 1971

I spent a lot of time with my mate Dougie S, who also lived in High Knocke. He let me know about Mummy's death before anyone had told me. Not really the right way for a child to find out such profound and devastating news, but I believe in retrospect, I'd rather have been told by one of my compatriots. And as well as being a fairly tough lad and leading me in to a few scrapes, Dougie was also always honest with me.

And I was with Dougie on a glorious August big sky day, in the long hot summer of '73, sitting under a Dymchurch willow tree in his garden, that he suddenly asked ...**"Ever been to Dreamland John?"** Instantly, for a highly enthusiastic and passionate young boy of 11 years old, the name "Dreamland" in itself conjured up joy and excitement of potentially mythical status!
"Noooo" I said, "Where is thaaaat?" "A place called Margate" answered Dougie. "And it's the greatest funfair in the whole of England!" "Wow!" I exclaimed. "What's the ghost train like?" "Much bigger than ours in Dymchurch" he replied. "Actually the scariest and longest ghost train in the whole world!" (the world at that time didn't extend much beyond the local area of Romney Marsh). Dougie then proceeded to describe in great detail a massive and special place of pure enchantment, magic and fun. I was wide-eyed and sold! **And in my dreams I dreamed of Dreamland.**
I imagined riding the ghost train and the most wild and crazy rollercoasters. The rock n' roll music and the

dodgems, the scenic railway and the magnificent big wheel. The buzz, bells and tunes from fruit machines of every conceivable kind and especially his wild wizardry favourites – a massive selection of the best pinball machines on the planet. Most of all, I thought it must be a place filled with endless laughter and fun, and especially pretty girls in pretty clothes and smiling happy people. In my heart I knew I would go there one day. When that might be, I could not know (and time moves differently for a child); but even at this early stage, my heart spoke words of truth to me. **I was a very bright and perceptive boy.**

It was also the summer of 1973, I reluctantly left Dymchurch Primary and went to Southland's Comprehensive in New Romney for the first-year seniors. (**Now called year 7*). My Dad hadn't done me any favours by informing me that "I would be going from being a big fish in a small pool, to a small fish in a big pool". I was certainly not enamoured by this prospect.

It turned out to be OK, although I experienced some nasty bullying, and by now there was mounting pressures at home. Mummy's death had deeply affected the whole family; and the overwhelming pressures on my brave sister were taking their toll on

her health and well-being. And also for my Dad, who had obviously been deeply affected by the death of his wife, his mother and his cat, all in such a short space of time. 😢
So in the end, the whole situation became untenable and my sister needed to move on in order to fulfil her own destiny and God's Plan for her. Alas, my Father took her departure very badly and was never in a good place about it, becoming sad and embittered. 😔
So in the June of 74 we were taken out of school (literally overnight) and packed off to our Auntie Peggy in Ickenham, London, whilst my Father decided what to do. We spent an amazing month with our dear Auntie (who had actually been Mummy's best friend and was always a sunny joyous person), and her lovely grown-up daughters Helen and Hazel. She took us on holiday to Bournemouth (saw the iconic 74 World Cup Final live too – Germany 4 v Holland 1) and also my first visit to a London Theatre.
But despite creating these special memories, still the air was filled with uncertainty and worry. Where would we be going next? Would we be going back home? My life and all my friends were there on Romney Marsh. But I couldn't be sure. Our Dad had always been a somewhat single-minded and secretive man, and by now he must have been feeling deep hurt and brokenness; so neither myself, nor indeed Auntie Peggy were told anything. Goodbye innocence. Goodbye old life! 😢

Summer 74 – Eastry Children's Home

On Saturday July 20th 1974, on a scorching hot summer's day a week and a half before my 12th birthday, Dad collected us in his old Hillman, sadly refused to tell Auntie Peggy where he was taking us, and began the drive South. Just outside London he announced that we would not be going back home, as there was 'no one there' to look after us and he couldn't cope. So we were to be temporarily separated. My youngest brother and little sister would be going to a place called Birchington, whilst my brother Bill and I would be going to a place called Eastry, near Dover, deep in the Kent countryside. He hoped we would be reunited with our younger siblings at a later date soon. 🙏 I can recall the feeling of absolute trepidation and the shock of being told we would be separated. For a good part of the journey, I tried very hard and with tenacious persistence, to persuade Dad that this was a bad idea and he should take us home. That we could manage if we all stuck together. But obviously, he'd already signed us over to the Kent County Council. In retrospect, I have no doubt this was the best thing he could have done for us, but obviously on that sad and fateful day, the prospect of strangers, children's homes and separation from each other and all we'd ever known, appeared to be the new 'nightmare scenario',

following Mummy's death 4 years earlier.
There's a moment on the journey South in to Kent where the journey splits. You can take the M20, which takes you to Folkestone and the Romney Marsh; or you can take the M2, which takes you to North Kent and the Isle of Thanet (Birchington and Margate). Of course, Dad took this road. At this moment I knew there was no turning back. I believe I was silent for the rest of the journey. **It is with the fullness of faith and retrospective, that I can now say with absolute certainty that my Father made the correct decision that day, and WAS doing what he believed to be his best for the welfare of his children.*
We dropped my little sister Lizzie and youngest brother Edward, at Spurgeons Homes for Children in Birchington. It seemed like a real clean and decent place with a most affable houseparent called Barbara Harris; but we were about to leave our siblings behind, so this all went by in a misty blur. There then followed the 12-mile journey to Eastry for myself and my brother Bill. I knew he was scared and I was determined to protect him. But I was filled with fear and foreboding myself.
We eventually drove up this tiny dark country lane and finally beneath an imposing arch to a group of council owned cottage homes. The imposing sign read 'Eastry Children's Home'. I believe I took a very large breath at that moment and I could feel my younger brother's terror. No getting out of it now! ☹

We moved in to one Lime Cottage with husband-and-wife house-parents ('Uncle' Brian and 'Auntie' Jan - probably in their late 30's/early 40's – who seemed decent enough, if a little rough and ready), and an imposing and harsh looking Scottish woman we were told to call 'Auntie' Mary. She was certainly no Auntie! There was also a young houseparent – a huge guy in his early 30's. We met the other 9 or 10 boys (an all-boys house), who were a mixture of ages from 15 down to around 9 (so my brother Bill would be one of the youngest). The first night I remember as possibly the scariest night of my life. We were in a large attic dormitory – there must have been 11 or 12 of us. I literally lay there in a bed and pissed myself with fear. I wasn't alone. All the boys except the very oldest also

wet their beds every night. These were seriously broken and damaged children. I also made a vow that night that I would no longer trust adults fully – ever again. That I would make my own decisions wherever possible. I felt abandoned and very alone and I can only imagine how scared my little brother was. I awoke that first morning in my own soaking wet bed and the stench of piss and excrement all around me. But even in these circumstances, I was already determined to make the best of it. This has always been my way. Fortunately for me and my brother, we had arrived at a moment in the school holidays where the home were planning a holiday trip to Pontins – Camber Sands for the following week. This would also coincide with my 12th Birthday, so it felt like an opportunity. I always remember that holiday with some joy. Proper 'old school 'Hi de hi!' and great fun. A shining light in the midst of a very dark time. On returning to the home, I settled down to life in 'care' and surviving the bullies and toughness of it all. The houseparent by the standards of those days was Ok. He did have compassion and a generally good nature; but these were the days of corporal punishment, so he would delight in telling us all that he was "paid good money to belt kids!" So called 'Auntie' Mary was just cruel – "I'll draw my hand across your damn face Laddie!"
I tried to protect my little brother at all times, but I was only little myself and hadn't learned how to physically fight at that stage of my life. Moreover, on the second

day in Eastry, I broke my wrist playing football. Then as soon as it was out of plaster, I broke it again doing Judo. There was no safeguarding, health and safety nor 'pandering' to children back then. I was getting seriously toughened up. Indeed, often we were lined up and given the slipper, just in case we were naughty! We invariably were – bunch of 'ragamuffins' we were!
I also got in to a serious disagreement over my forthcoming schooling for the next term. Because all the children of secondary school age went to the local secondary modern, I was told I would be attending there. However, I had passed my 11+ with absolute 'flying colours' (in the 90%'s), so I was not about to submit to that injustice. I kicked up 'merry hell' and the powers that be were forced to send me to Dover Grammar School. Great school, but at that time it was a real struggle for me, with an arm in plaster, away from all my family and friends and my education already disrupted.
One day I could take no more; so I ran away back to the Romney Marsh, arriving on the Saltwood doorstep of dear family friends Joan and David Wiggell, late in the afternoon. They were kind and understanding and it was arranged that we could go and stay at their home at weekends; myself and my brother one week and my little sister and youngest brother another week. These were happy weekends, but alas, they didn't last. Never fully knew why, but I think Dad had a fall-out with them, so that was that. ☹

Alas, my Dad was not in a good place at this time. No one 'fought' more with him than I, no one questioned him more than I, and no one resented him more than I. ** I always tried to get on with him, and these days, I try to put myself in his shoes; having lost his wife, his Mum, his black cat, and then my half-sister departing – all in the space of only 4 years.*
Now it was autumn and the school term began. I made the best of everything I could, but in truth, the school was imposing and demanding and I just felt vulnerable and unsettled. Especially as I was now pressing hard for us to join our little sister and brother in Birchington. Soon the opportunity arose that we could join them and I was 'over the moon'! ☽

Dover Grammar School

Autumn 74 – Spurgeon's Homes For Children

So it came to pass that I found myself arriving at Spurgeons Homes for Children – Birchington (near Margate) one cool crisp autumnal day. **It was October 30th 1974 – Halloween Eve,** during half-term. I was a little battered to be honest; my double-broken right wrist still heavily in plaster (I'm very right-handed), my emotions in tatters after the traumatic events of the summer, homesick for Romney Marsh and missing my Dymchurch friends and my big sisters. Moreover, in serious need of some safety and respite.

Spurgeon's Homes was a unique and special independent Baptist Children's home, situated in the village of Birchington-on-Sea on the Isle of Thanet, in the North-East part of Kent.

Close to famous holiday resorts of Margate, Westgate, Broadstairs and Ramsgate, it was a magical area to bring up children, especially through the 50's, 60's and 70's. The home was opened in 1951, as a brand-new state of the art premises, following previous homes in Reigate and in London. Spurgeons was founded in 1867 by one of the most well-known public figures of the day – a Baptist preacher and author called Charles Haddon Spurgeon. He founded an orphanage in Stockwell, south London, which really thrived and helped hundreds of orphans. A large number of the children who were taken in were suffering from bad health and so it was decided to open a home by the sea where the children could enjoy a holiday and regain their health. Eventually a large house was purchased in Northdown Road, Cliftonville, which was also used as a primary school. And in 1917 the Stockwell Orphanage celebrated its 50-year anniversary at the Queen's Hall in London. To celebrate this event, it was decided to establish another seaside home and Birchington Hall and it's 40 acres of farmland were purchased in 1922, and the Margate children moved there. Just prior to World War II, another home was purchased at Reigate, and with the outbreak of the war, the children were all evacuated there.

By the end of the war the Stockwell orphanage was old and badly damaged and the Reigate site was no longer suitable, so the farm land at Birchington was developed and by 1953, all the children had moved in to their new and healthy home by the sea. It comprised of an exclusive home for babies and toddlers and 3 blocks of 4 houses, all named after prominent places and people from Spurgeon's history. Each house catered for up to 18 children under the care of 2 house parents. The cooking, gardening and cleaning were undertaken by a band of paid locals who came in faithfully each day. Each block had its own dedicated kitchens. There were large sprawling grounds with finely mowed lawns and sumptuous cultivated roses. There was a most beautiful chapel, a lodge (known as sick bay), its own stores, walled garden, tennis courts, a sports pavilion with a stage, adjacent to a large playing field. And where the old Birchington Hall once stood, there remained large majestic trees; yew, birch, sycamores and cypress. It was an impressive place.

Spurgeon's Homes – Birchington – 1970's

Our particular house was aptly called Stockwell and it was a mixture of children; the 4 of us Lowdells, two older teenage girls – Peto H and Susan B and her 2 younger sisters Sharon and Karen, and a couple of younger children also – The Coopers. I was the eldest boy at 12. So I believe there were ten of us in total.

This rare picture of myself and my 3 younger siblings with the 2 house parents Barbara Harris (Auntie Barbara) and Margaret Buckley, was taken outside of "Stockwell" on the day we arrived. My little sister looks so happy (very rare for her in those days). It's clear she was very relieved to be reunited with her big brothers; and the feeling was mutual!

The first thing I noticed about the house was how clean everything was. It seemed very clinical to me then and thus a little intimidating. Barbara kept such a ship-shape house and there was no messing with her regime. She was a most forthright Welsh lady from Swansea, with old school values, strict cleanliness and a code of honour that let the children know what was right and what was wrong. But although I had many run-ins with her (as a highly intense, troubled and argumentative teenager), she always tried to be fair and most importantly, she had a kind heart which shone through. She was smart in dress and attitude, which I respected her for. Her assistant Margaret was a kind, sensitive and gentle-hearted lady from Derbyshire. She was far 'softer' on us than Barbara, which I am 'ashamed' to say I would go on to take full advantage of in playing her up!

But I'd not been used to a house like this – with polished floors so clean you could see your face in them. The light shone bright through the large windows and Barbara would not tolerate a speck of dust to flitter in those searching beams! The airing cupboard was full of warm fresh linen, with a sweet aroma of cleanliness I can remember and detect in my nostrils to this very day. 😊

Meals were served in a large dining room, with an annexe leading through to a large kitchen which served 2 houses with professional cooks.

We were most fortunate to have the amazing Dorothy Fairbrother as our cook. **She would in later years foster me from the home (but that's another story).* The food was of high quality (very different from the council run orphanage at Eastry). And that first night we had fish fingers and a lovely pudding. And as it was half-term and my first night, I was allowed to stay up and watch the big fight between Ali and Foreman (the famous 'Rumble in the Jungle'). This was a great start for my relationship with my new House Parent. She was from a long line of tough and solid Welsh stock, so no doubt appreciated a good scrap! But most importantly, that auspicious night - she knew she had a proper competitive and combative minded young boy in her care, and was prepared to nurture this. Barbara's kindness that night, reminded me of how shortly before my Mummy died, she had the foresight to introduce her 7½ year old to football by letting me stay up and watch the infamous 1970 Cup Final replay between Chelsea and Leeds. I became an Arsenal boy of course, but nevertheless, the football match (or should I say battle?) on that particular night was life-defining. This felt similar to me in terms of having a friend and ally, like I used to have.
Barbara also told me that I would be going out to Broadstairs the next day with the home's principal – John Honey, to be fitted with my school uniform.
So I felt excited as I went up to bed on that first night in Spurgeons. 😁

There were a couple of individual rooms for the older girls and then a couple of dormitories, one for the girls and one for the boys. I was in a large room with my two younger brothers (Bill and Eddie). The beds were immaculately made with crisp white super clean sheets, folded with ‘envelope’ corners.
And at the bottom was fitted the bed-wetting plastic sheet. Obviously, the homes would have been informed in advance. But somehow, I already knew. I wouldn’t be needing it again. Firstly, would I dare to wet the bed and soil such cleanliness? No, I couldn’t do that. Despite being incredibly wilful and argumentative, I was always a child who desired to please. Secondly, I was in a house with nice young girls – and I always loved the girls and never wanted to be shown up in front of them. No – I couldn’t do that! 😲
But most importantly, both consciously and subconsciously, I now felt safe and protected and, in an environment where I could breathe again, reunited with my younger siblings, in a house of really pleasant kids. So finally, an end of my horrible enuresis – permanently. 🙏
So I was delighted and very proud of myself to wake up on that first morning with a dry bed (the first time in months) and all kinds of possibilities in my new home. Barbara would be like a ‘regimental soldier’ in the morning – moving at some speed, ripping open the curtains and getting us moving quickly and efficiently with orders to *“pull those covers right back!”*

“Down the corridor – get washed - downstairs in 10 minutes!” There was no hanging around! Morning prayers then breakfast. I have to admit I found this all a bit challenging, being a lazy lion in the mornings – but I have no doubt in retrospect, this discipline did me the world of good. That first excellent breakfast I met the wonderful and friendly cook, and we warmed to each other immediately. After that I would always greet her with “Good Morning Mrs.Fairbrother – how are you today?” She loved the fact that I was so well-mannered, just like I’d been taught. *I have always enjoyed being charming and making other’s smile – this characteristic in me has never been fake, it’s always from the heart.* 💖
So it was this Halloween day I got to meet the Principal of the Homes, John Honey - who took me to Broadstairs to get my school uniform. This was a happy day. It wasn’t scary at all. I had been granted a place at Chatham House Grammar School For Boys in Ramsgate; a historic and traditional school of high standards and repute, where the Prime Minister Edward Heath had attended. So choosing my smart new green uniform was a delight. Moreover, John Honey was a true old-fashioned gentleman. He was caring, empathetic and kind; but strict and stern at the same time, if he needed to be. I warmed to him immediately and was eager not to disappoint him. For reasons unknown (‘cos I met some smart kids in the Spurgeons), I was the only boy in the home to be

attending the grammar school, so he was obviously very proud of me. I know it may sound a little elitist by today's ideals and I don't really like snobbery; but in those days, much was made of which school a child attended. Afterwards, 'Uncle' John took me to the Wimpy in Margate and I also had my very first **Knickerbocker Glory** – yum! yum! So I was here – THIS was Margate – and here was **Dreamland!** I'd arrived. I thought of my old mate Dougie back in Dymchurch – *"I'm Here Mate!"*

I was due to start school on the coming Monday, but before this I experienced my first weekend in the homes, where I met some of the other children from the different houses. On the Saturday parents or relatives would come to take the children out and Dad would do the same with us. Occasionally, we would go and visit our lovely old Grandpa George in Canterbury, but this wasn't often as Dad didn't get on particularly well with his own Dad! So his favoured place was the hoverport and beach at Pegwell Bay in Ramsgate. It was always good to go out together as a little family, although relations were often challenging between myself and Dad. I would argue with him more and more as I was growing up and becoming my own man. But at 12 years old, although I always had lots to say, I didn't have much of a say, even though as his eldest son, I liked to think I did. To be fair, he did occasionally consult me on matters. Although I don't recall many times him actually heeding any of my advice!

A shame really – I was an observant and discerning kid for one so young. But I was also extremely sensitive, with a very sharp mind; and more than a little OCD, so I often took things personally and was easily hurt.
**I suppose these days there would be a label or some kind of acronym for this!* 😉

With brother Bill – Pegwell Bay - 1975

As Spurgeons' was an independent home with strict Baptist values that underpinned their whole ethos, we had to go to church twice on a Sunday. Different local Baptist churches in the morning (ours was Birchington) and Spurgeons' own chapel within the grounds in the evening. There was a strict smart dress code and best behaviour was mandatory. I intensely disliked marching down to the church through the village square in the morning with the rest of Stockwell House. Too regimented for me – felt like I was being 'robbed' of my individuality!

**I've always been a dedicated individual – for me individuality is the ultimate identity.* I also disliked the claustrophobic, sanitized church, with bare scrubbed walls and windows, without stain glass, decoration, nor ornate Christian imagery. I'd grown up with the pageantry and symbolism of the Church of England, with its ancient traditional churches and glorious historic splendour. And what were these 'dry as dust' uninspiring sermons that went on and on and on in a monotone voice, boring me to distraction? I found it excruciating!

The Sunday evening chapel services were a very different dynamic. The chapel was large, modern, spacious and all together more splendid. Moreover, this was the service where every child in the home was expected to attend and all the houseparents, principal and main staff were there. This was a service for everyone – no exemptions. John Honey would give an excellent reading and we would all sing the hymns. And one of the first things I noticed were there were all kinds of different children, including black children, whom I'd never seen before, let alone met. *I enjoyed immediately becoming friends with children of different areas, backgrounds, cultures and stories. In truth, I've never understood racism or prejudice of any kind. In the home, we were all in the same 'ship', all with our own problems, but we all bled red.*

And in those early chapel services in late 1974, we would also notice one another and I soon got the occasional sweet little smiles from the one or two of the girls my age. So it wasn't long before I had my first 'child girlfriend' to have my first 'proper' kiss with – one Delia from Birmingham (the younger sister of my housemate Peto). I think we lasted 2 or 3 weeks (felt like months at that age! 😉 I also quickly started to make some good friends, especially one David M, who was actually 3 years older than me and had actually been in the homes since he was a baby. I am close friends with David to this day.

The Beautiful Chapel – Spurgeon's Homes

In the future it would be demolished for housing. Sacrilege really + the acoustics were magnificent!

November 4th 1974 – Welcome to Chatham House

So early on a rainy cold Monday morning, I arrived smartly at my foreboding, grand and gothic school on a hill in Chatham Street, Ramsgate.

The bus journey was long, but engaging for that reason – especially as we had to change at Margate. I was there again! Although Margate in the winter is a very different 'beast' to Margate in the summer, when the freezing Easterly winds would roar across the North Sea to chill the bones. I also quickly got chatting with other boys on the bus and met one Ian P on the first day – a massive Elton John fan and dedicated music connoisseur like me; and also a very well mannered,

super bright and friendly young man. He was instantly welcoming to me.
The very first lesson on the very first day resulted in my getting punched in the face. I took my seat at the front, in a freezing stone attic classroom for double Maths (yikes!) A big and bold lad entered the room and told me that this was his seat and so I had to move. When I refused, he immediately punched me in the face! 👊
It was one Russell P, a highly intelligent lad, but also a 'hard as nails' Spurs football hooligan (even at that age!) He must have instinctively known I was Arsenal fan, but this was 'Welcome to Chatham House' - a tough and competitive all boy's environment, where you're going to have to be strong to 'survive and thrive'! At the time I was most insulted, but looking back, I'm grateful to Russ for teaching me such a valuable lesson so early, and we became good mates, despite the rivalry.
I was at that time very small and skinny, as I was almost the youngest boy in my year as an August birthday. Boys like Russ were almost a year ahead of me in physical growth. Anyway, I survived double Maths and my first day, despite a sore chin and a mad old teacher with a habit of throwing the blackboard rubber at insolent young boys. I had some very interesting lessons with academic and eccentric teachers still wearing their university black coats and mortarboards. And I quickly made friends too – mostly football, music and girl loving healthy young boys like

myself – all fairly clever, all competitive, and mostly all pleasant. It would be fair to say that despite a turbulent first day and feeling somewhat vulnerable with a broken arm and unable to write properly with my left hand, I enjoyed the first week in my new school. It seemed so full of potential and I was determined to catch up and prosper after all the disruptions to my schooling. And did I 'grass up' Russ to the teachers or complain when I got home? Absolutely not! We had code of honour in those days, which did not include 'grassing'! 👌

Chatham House was a highly competitive sporty school with an extensive curriculum. I've always loved sport of all kinds; rugby, football, cricket, tennis, boxing, martial arts, athletics, golf, horse racing, snooker and chess. ♟

It had an 8-house system with a different colour tie for each, a house master and a structured and organized hierarchy beneath. (I was in Searles' / red tie). There was proper rivalry between the houses. There were all sorts of competitions and cups throughout the school year. For hockey, cricket, rugby and athletics. And all sorts of school societies that mirrored the great university models. A debating society, a thespian society, chess club, school political groups, and so on and so forth. And this was a school that sat the Oxbridge exam, once a pupil reached a certain age. Perhaps here was a school where I could finally settle, and maybe even excel. 🖖

Friday November 8th 1974 – Birchington Village Centre

During my first week, Auntie Barbara asked me if I would like to go to the kids disco on Friday. This was at the Birchington Village Centre and it was effectively an under-18 affair, where I would actually be one of the youngest. The truth is I'd never been to a disco before and the idea was very exciting!
Dear Barbara could not have known then how significant a moment this actually was and how this one venue would change my life forever! ✨
She also told me that one afternoon when I got home from school, she would take me to the special clothes and shoe shop in Birchington, to choose some new trousers, shirt and shoes for this auspicious occasion. So I chose crepe shoes ('all the rage' in 74), a wide collared white shirt with vintage cars on it, and some very fashionable blue flares. I also purchased some Brut 33, so I would smell awesome; like our own very heavyweight champ Henry Cooper – who was advertising it at the time as "splash it on all over!" And I did! 😉
So on the Friday after my first week at school, I attended my first disco with some of my new friends. And I absolutely loved it. The 70's music and the lights (although I recall it being very dark), the buzzing atmosphere and most of all the pretty girls dancing to the great disco songs of the time – "Rock you Baby" - George Macrae, The Stylistics, Kool and the Gang, and

of course - Hues Corporation – “Rock the Boat” – for which we learned a special dance. Most of all I loved the great hit by Mud – “Tiger Feet” – for which we also had our own dedicated dance; and for which my new crepe shoes had been invented!
And I also learned early, that one of the main objectives of the evening was to ‘pluck up’ the courage to ask a girl to dance to a slow one – probably “The way we were” by Barbara Streisand, which was the biggest hit of that year. To ask a girl to dance – now that took a new level of bravado; which although very shy at that age, I soon acquired the art of; although simulating confidence I didn’t really possess! They didn’t always say “yes”, but for a ‘good-looking’ young man like myself – they often did! 😉 And so my confidence grew a little bit. From then on, the Birchington disco would become the highlight of my week, and my main social scene. It’s also where I learned those interactions between boys and girls – the nuances, the posturing, the shyness and awkwardness of youth and innocence; how to dance, what to say and what not to say and most of all – those first innocent kisses. This was my place of social education with the opposite sex, and I loved it. I also dreamed of meeting the perfect girl for me. **Maybe someone who looked like one of the beautiful girls from the new Swedish Eurovision winners – ABBA? Yeah right – in my dreams!!** 🙄

Frida & Agnetha
ABBA Tour - 1979

1975 – 1977 – Growing up

"Is it me, for a moment...
Bell boy... Love, reign o'er me...
Can you see the real me, can you, can you?"

Pete Townshend – "THE WHO – I Am the Sea"

Moon Over Walpole Bay © John Hinde Collection

So in the latter part of 1974 and early 1975, I was settling in well in the homes and at school. I continued to make good friends, at the homes and at school. I'd also joined 1st Birchington Scouts, run by a wonderful guy named Bryan Southern, who was also a good mentor for me. And I loved outdoor activities – camping, trekking, abseiling, sports. *Scouts was such a wonderful grounding for us boys. I notice Bear Grylls still wears his scouts' badge with pride.*

And as children in care, the houseparents had to write regular reports about us. Overleaf is an extract from my first report from the start of 1975: -

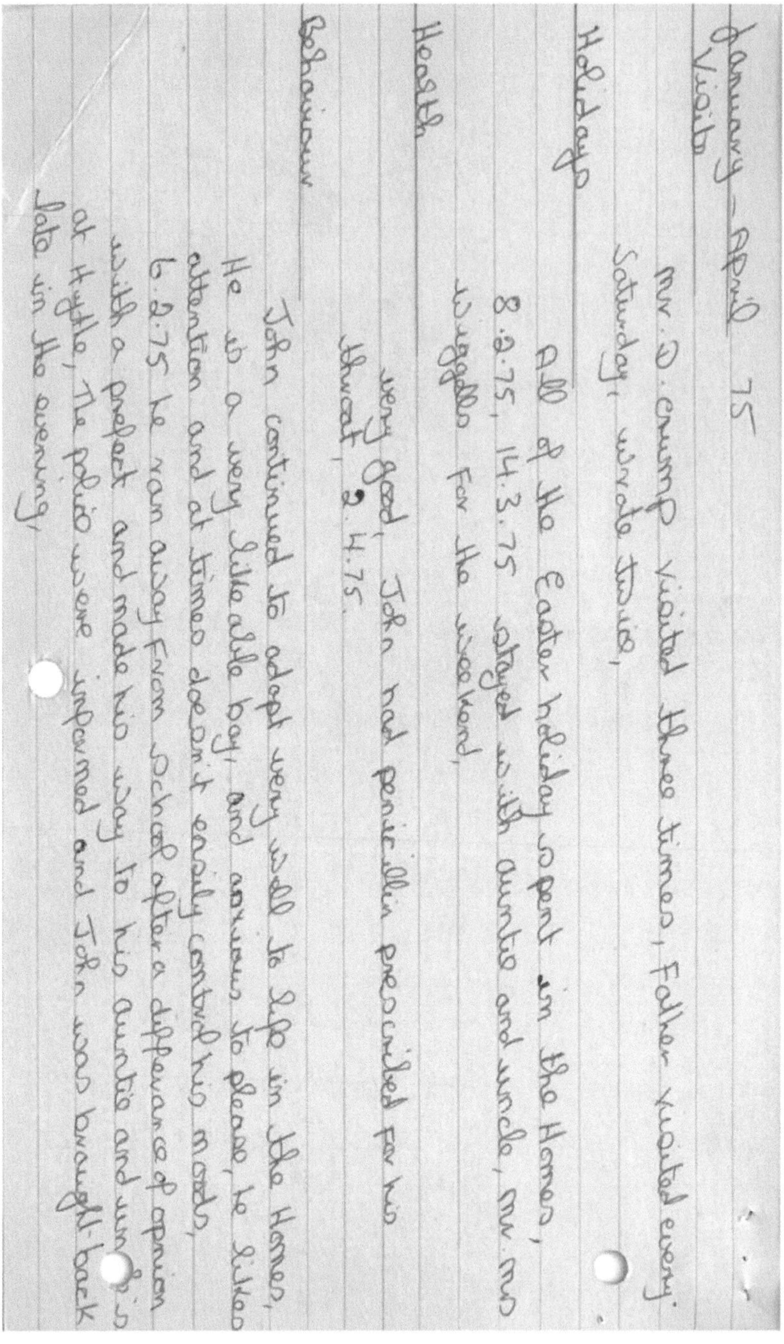

January – April 75
Visits
Mr. D. Crump visited three times, Father visited every Saturday, wrote twice,
Holidays
All of the Easter holiday spent in the Homes,
8.2.75, 14.3.75 stayed with auntie and uncle, Mr. Mrs Wiggells for the weekend,
Health
very good, John had penicillin prescribed for his throat, 2.4.75.
Behaviour
John continued to adopt very well to life in the Homes, He is a very likeable boy, and anxious to please, he likes attention and at times doesn't easily control his moods,
6.2.75 he ran away from school after a differance of opnion with a prefect and made his way to his auntie and uncle's at Hythe, The police were informed and John was brought back late in the evening,

This was actually one of several 'runaway' incidents. I was constantly disagreeing and arguing with my Dad and was especially upset after he put our family cats

Mij and Florence in to homes too, which broke my heart, as I never saw them again, nor knew what happened to them. This was a cruel thing to do. **To this day, I have serious aversion to anyone who gives a cat away.* It's not like he didn't have the room. ☹ Also sadly in August 1976, our dear old Grandpa passed away; but we never got to go to any funeral, nor any information where he was actually buried.

I really felt at this point that Dad had 'lost the plot'. I got very fed up with the constant secrecy and the 'need to know' basis that he (and others), would bring to bear upon me. **I used to consider that kind of behaviour a form of dishonesty, which really disturbed me; as honesty was, and still remains, an attribute most important to me.*

So I wanted to show him and the other adults of my world that I wouldn't just accept anything they wanted to do, nor could I be held down or contained; that I was a free spirit and knew my own mind – even at such a young age. And though I was punished for it, this made me even more determined to exert my individuality and bravado. 💪 There was also a certain 'street cred' in 'doing a runner' (as it was called!) I also took up smoking, which I actually loved. **Took over 30 years to quit tobacco!* But in all truth, the rebellion was often in conflict with my inherent willingness to please and to do well. So clearly I was a disturbed young boy, deeply affected by the breakdown of my family home and my Mother's death. Although I did find it both curious and amusing when reading the report, to see at such an early age such a behavioural microcosm of my character for life – an adaptable, likeable, amiable show-off! Moody, rebellious, strong-willed and defiant. *Thank you Barbara. You'd sussed me pretty quick!* What Barbara didn't say on this report is possibly the most important part of all – that she took me (along with my brother Bill), to my first Arsenal match on 15th Feb 1975 – Leicester at Home in the FA Cup 5th Round, and we stood down the front of the North Bank. It was 0-0 (it often was in those days!), but nevertheless, fair play to her. After all, my Dad hated football! 😳 And in return for good behaviour, she took me again at the end of April to my first Arsenal v Tottenham game. And this time we won 1-0. 😊

I am eternally grateful to Barbara for taking me to my first of so many games, that I've lost count of in 52 years of supporting the Gunners. And especially to my first game against Spurs, where I also witnessed pitched terrace battles going on across the clock end – yes those were the days! (or maybe not?!) 😉

And as I became a teenager that year, it's illuminating to see my houseparents report overleaf from September '75 –

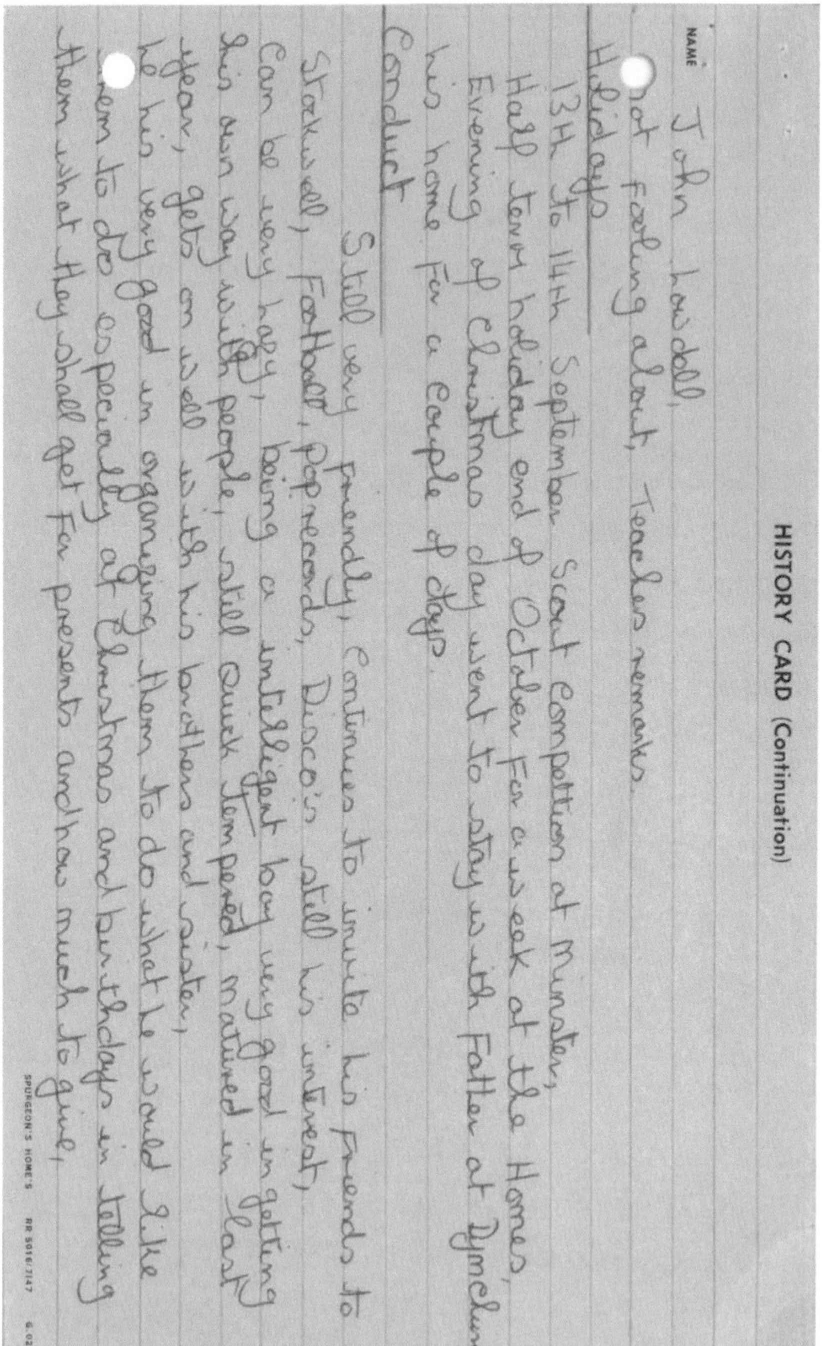

HISTORY CARD (Continuation)

NAME John Lowdell,

not fooling about, Teachers remarks.

Holidays

13th to 14th September Scout competition at Minster,

Half term holiday end of October for a week at the Homes,

Evening of Christmas day went to stay with Father at Dymchurch his home for a couple of days.

Conduct

Still very friendly, continues to invite his friends to Stockwell, Football, pop records, Disco's still his interest,

Can be very lazy, being a intelligent boy very good in getting his own way with people, still quick tempered, matured in last year, gets on well with his brothers and sister,

he his very good in organizing them to do what he would like them to do especially at Christmas and birthdays in telling them what they shall get for presents and how much to give,

SPURGEON'S HOME'S RR 5016/7147 G.0204

**The first part from school reads "John's work has improved over the year, but could work a lot harder*

when he is … not fooling about …” I was always playing the fool to be honest, (I’ve always enjoyed to make people laugh); and after all, as well as a natural show-off, I was a natural showman _(*which Jayl proved later);_ and anything for the attention! 🙄 And thus further comments from Barbara are again well observed - of a friendly, popular and intelligent boy; but sometimes lazy, quick tempered and bossy. Loving football, music, records, discos and girls! _*To be fair, astrologically speaking, I have always been a proper Leo Lion, and this was also very obvious in my early life. So tis true I can sometimes be a lazy lion, sometimes a ferocious lion and often a dominant lion. 🦁 But I have needed these attributes to survive and thrive in this world. And as my ladies and closest friends will no doubt testify, I also have the heart of a lion and the loyalty of a lion. And most importantly, beneath it all, they know I’m really just a shy and loving pussy cat!_ 😉 The latter part of 1975 and in to early 1976, I really settled down to life in Spurgeon’s and despite my Dad advertising for housekeepers, (holding out hope that we could return to the family home), I had no belief in this ideal; nor would I have been prepared to move again. Alas, the uncertainty took its toll sometimes; I was a capricious boy, and I was now often in trouble at school for messing around, cheekiness or fighting, and consequently had many detentions. It’s fair to say I was challenging the ‘system’. On the outside I enjoyed pushing it, and it brought me attention as well as detention; but inside I was hurting and hated myself for it. ☹ In this respect, it was just another form of personal conflict, essentially mental self-harm and self-deprecation, which I often suffered from. I received some counselling at school from one of the teachers – a kind and caring man named Roger N, who helped as much as he could; but inevitably I suffered lots of bullying. And being one of the youngest kids in the year, I wasn't tough enough to fight back properly, although I always tried to stand my ground and prided myself on always getting back up. Most of the problem was simply immaturity, with the uncertainties and insecurities that come with it. However, at that time I had a massive growth spurt, from about 5ft 0 – to a skinny 6-footer, and started to mature a lot and feel a bit more like a young man. My houseparent reports overleaf from May – Sept 1976 reflects this: -

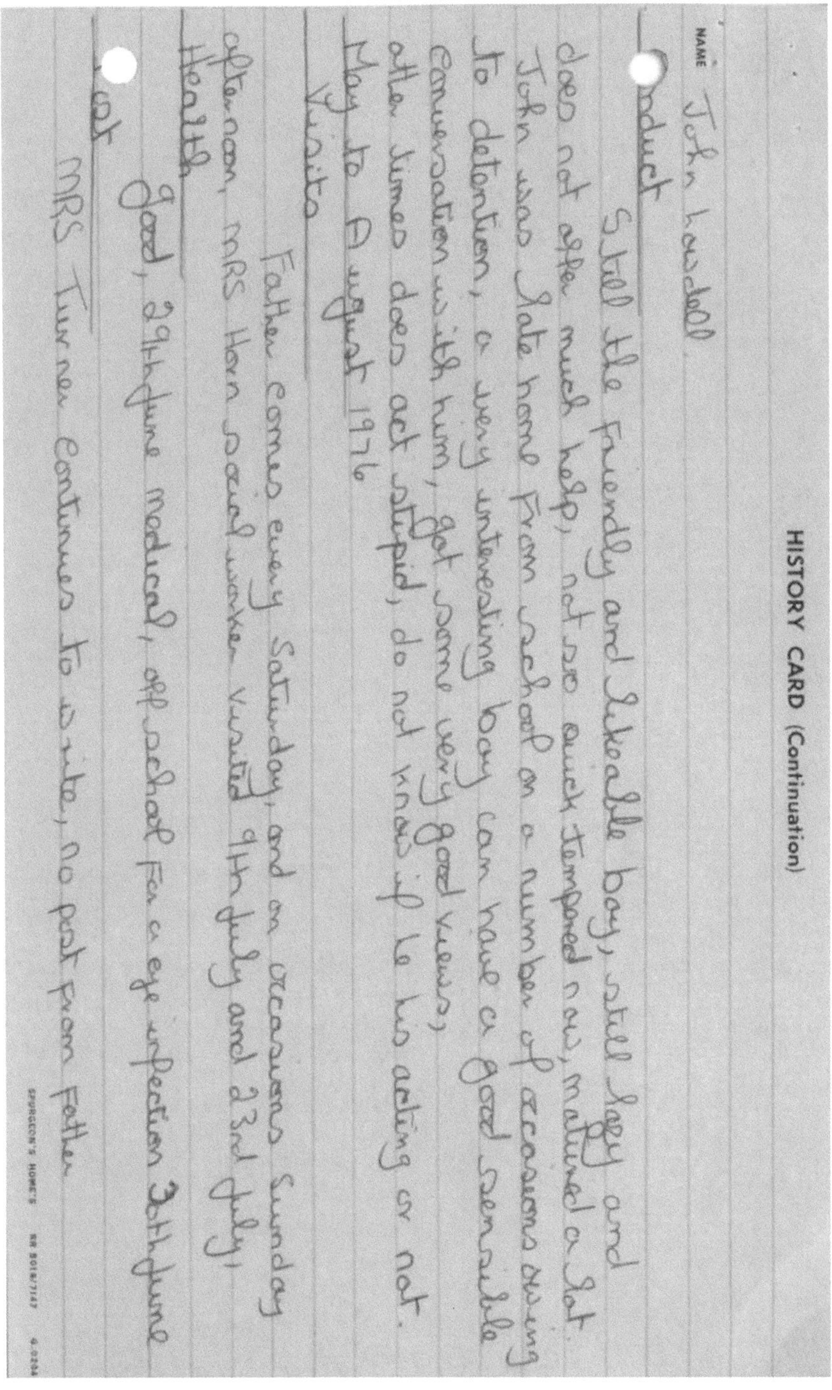

HISTORY CARD (Continuation)

NAME John Lowdell

Conduct

Still the friendly and likeable boy, still lazy and does not offer much help, not so quick tempered now, matured a lot. John was late home from school on a number of occasions owing to detention, a very interesting boy can have a good sensible conversation with him, got some very good views, other times does act stupid, do not know if he his acting or not.

May to August 1976

Visits

Father comes every Saturday, and on occasions Sunday afternoon, MRS Horn social worker visited 9th July and 23rd July,

Health

Good, 29th June medical, off school for a eye infection 30th June

Post

MRS Turner continues to write, no post from Father

SPURGEON'S HOME'S RR 5018/7147 G.0204

*Funny to note Barbara contemplating whilst I was playing the fool, whether I "was acting or not". 🤣

Now Barbara – you've been waiting many years to hear this, so yes, I ***was*** *acting! My apologies – I always have tried it on! If I could get away with it!* 😉

The second part of the report is notable firstly, for my going to the disco in defiance of my punishment for rudeness. But 'wild horses' would not have prevented me going to the Birchington Village Centre Disco, especially as I had just met a lovely girl at the previous disco, who had already become my first 'official' serious girlfriend – one Deborah (a St.George's schoolgirl – an excellent local school in Broadstairs), and I was fairly besotted with her.

Deborah (*Deb for short*), was a mysterious late October girl, so although in the same year as me, she was 14½, with me still essentially only 13½. At that age this can manifest as a significant age difference, especially as girls mature faster than boys and Deborah seemed very grown-up. But I was keen to be a great boyfriend and we got on very well. I would share my problems with her and she would attentively listen.

Also, her Mum, Dad and Grandma welcomed me in to their homes. However, I do recall to this very day the excruciating shyness that I used to feel because I wasn't sure what I was supposed to be doing. To be fair, Deborah, was patient and kind, so I could develop at my own pace. I felt much stronger in myself now having a lovely girlfriend. I believe I loved her; but as I was an absolute beginner, a little messed up, and didn't really know what love was at that stage, I wasn't able to show my feelings properly. But to this day, I remember Deb with great fondness and respect. 💖

May 1976 – Part 2

Holidays

28th May Scout Camp for weekend, 26th July to 7th August, Camp with Spurgeons to Keynsham, 19th August Germany with MR Honey and Bill on return to go to Brandon House ba[ck] to Stockwell 5th September,

Conduct, 3rd May

John on being teased by Miss Buckly was extremely rude to her, infront of another older boy, Margaret spoke to him about his behaviour he began to shout at her speaking in a disrespectful manner, he was told because of his behaviour he would not go to the disco on Saturday, he kept insisting he would go and nothing would stop him,

8th May. John went upstairs to his Room got himself ready and went to the disco, he did not return in the evening, he spent the night in the lodge,

8th June

John was seen in the afternoon in a amusement arca[de] in Margate, I spoke to him when he came home from school

Re: 'Conduct' **3rd May 76** – Nearly 14 by then, but no doubt showing-off. *"John was extremely rude to Miss Buckley in front of another older boy."* To be fair, the older boy was my friend David and also - I didn't really like being teased. But Ok, it's never too late for an apology, so Barbara (and Margaret B, if you ever happen to read this), I'm sorry. Nevertheless, I did have a very good reason – there WAS a young lady waiting for me! The final part of the above report reads: **8th June** *"John was seen in the afternoon in an amusement arcade in Margate* (*the one next to Dreamland actually). *I spoke to him when he came home from school* ... With the missing part reading ... *"He denied being there. John was seen by the headmaster the next day and was given a week's detention for playing truant. It was discovered this wasn't the first time."* Oh the lure of those fruit machines, the pinballs, the bells, lights and whistles! I was already a gambling addict (and also a cigarette addict) by the age of 14 and couldn't really get past a machine without playing it and smoking away whilst I was doing so. ☹ Moreover, Margate seafront was the half-way change buses route to and from school! Nevertheless, truancy is not the sign of an entirely contented child. However, I was always of a generally positive and happy disposition, so I tended to live in the moment and enjoy life. Furthermore, by becoming a bit of a 'bad boy', I believed it would impress my mates and especially the girls – at this juncture, my new girlfriend!

Finally, at the top of the above card it reads: -
"Holidays" - followed by a list of 4 different dates and places, including "Germany with Mr.Honey and Bill."
What it doesn't describe is that this was the famous long hot summer of 1976. ☼ And following the traumas and dramas of my 3rd year seniors and such rapid growing-up, that summer really gave me the chance to recuperate, reset, experience, and love life. And following a wonderful and fun-filled scout camp at Blean woods in Kent, I did OK in my exams and set about enjoying the magical summer. I spent a lot of time with Deb, and she came to the homes. She also came out with me and my Dad and siblings to the Hoverport at Pegwell Bay on his Saturday visits. I found myself getting on lots better with him as a consequence and looked forward to going out with him and my younger siblings. We mostly went to the same place, but I grew to love 'The Bay'.

Aged 14 - 1976

And what a summer - swimming, tennis, cinema (we called 'the pictures' back then), amusement arcades, Margate beach and of course **Dreamland!**
And the thrill of building my fast-expanding record collection and the education of Radio Caroline. Great music from 76 – the year of Bowie's "Station to Station" – "Golden Years", and Queen's seminal work -

"A Day at the Races"- "We will rock you!" I continued to collect The Beatles, now releasing some of their greatest work as solo artists, and especially Paul McCartney's WINGS. I also adored and collected the Rolling Stones, and used to study Mick Jagger closely! 🎤 My friend Francis J (a year older than me), was also a wonderful musical educator for me and would trustfully lend me his best albums (which I treated like 'gold'). He introduced me to bands that would become some of my greatest influences - Led Zeppelin, Pink Floyd, Genesis and Hawkwind. 🎸 But most importantly – The Who and their great iconic masterpiece

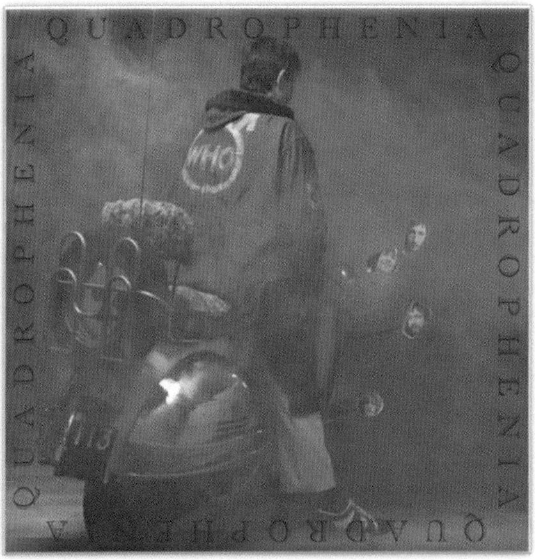

Quadrophenia; a life-changing album that I could truly relate to. The character in the story felt just like me – high-functioning, rebellious, lost and angry. And what fantastic compositions – with a sound ranging from the most sensitive and gentle ballads to a ferocious 'juggernaut' revving up when Keith Moon launched in to a frenzy on those drums. And as for Roger Daltrey – swinging that mic like a lethal weapon! And oh to be able to sing half as good as him! **Fortunately, one day I would*! 😉 🎤

I got my first job picking up litter in the homes for 50p a week (more than it sounds back then) and spent many happy times visiting and staying at mate's houses; especially my best mate at the time, Stevie B, who lived in Broadstairs near Deb. We would play football together, go to the arcades, listen to music and visit the clothes and record shops, and the wonderful Dumpton market. It was a magnificent summer! Famously HOT too! ☼ And after a fun trip to Keynsham with the homes, the rest of the holidays were spent at Brandon House, within the grounds – the residence of Principal John Honey. And in August my brother Bill and I with two other boys, were taken to Lahnstein (near Koblenz), Germany by Uncle John – the first time we'd ever been abroad or travelled on a Hovercraft across the channel. Such abiding and happy memories. He was such a kind and compassionate man and a natural with children. He was also a great mentor for myself and my younger brother and other kids too. We had to behave, but that was fine as we didn't wish to upset him and there was never cause to. He was traditionalist in his values, but also a moderniser and pioneer in childcare. Kindness was his mantra.

Burg Lahneck – Lahnstein - Germany

LIFE IN SPURGEONS

Early in my time at Spurgeons, in the Spring / Summer 75, John Honey had the dormitories within the houses turned in to individual small bedrooms for the older children, so my brother Bill and I now had adjacent bedrooms, rather than beds. To this day, I can still smell the distinct and delightful aroma of my brand-new private bedroom. This was a real sanctuary and I would spend a lot of time in my room.

New Bedrooms 1975 – With Bill - Arsenal v Leeds 😉

And in the following year of 76, it was awesome being trusted and allowed to take Deborah up to my room. We did lots of lovely kissing, cuddling and petting in that little room, but it was still all fairly innocent and 'above board'. Times were different then. We had been taught to treat girls with consideration and respect, and promiscuity was frowned upon in those days. I also didn't want to break Barbara's trust in me. I was already a proper young English Gent. 😊
Looking back now, we were just so fortunate to be in Spurgeons, as opposed to one of the many of the dangerous council run institutions of that time; after all we'd just come away from one such children's home. At Spurgeon's we were safe. Yes, there was strict discipline and a very strong emphasis on Baptist Christian values, but we were cared for, nurtured and loved. And there was a true camaraderie between the children in the homes. Every kid had their challenges, every kid was a little disturbed, every kid had a story. But judgementalism with each other was not really a thing. After all, we were taught Christian values that included "Judge not, lest thee be judged" and "Do unto others as you would have done to you" and the Lord's Prayer – "Forgive us our trespasses, as we forgive those who trespass against us."
Ok, many of us would fall short, and mumble the hymns and prayers. And it obviously wasn't cool for us to be in any way religious; but somehow, these simple but massively powerful precepts and ethics that

underpinned how we were with each other and how we were all Spurgeon's children – brothers and sisters by default, regardless of family, age, background or colour. We were all orphans of one kind or another, so were related by being in Spurgeons. And together we would put on magnificent pageants at Christmas, where we would present them to the public at the Winter Gardens in Margate and then at the Central Hall in Westminster. I clearly recall being Saul on the road to Damascus – Christmas 75. ✝️

And we would have a float which would be in the Birchington Carnival and in the sumptuous affair, which was the Margate Carnival. We would all dress up (often as street urchins with deep pockets 😉), and drive past hundreds of people, many of them throwing coins in to our float. There was always so much fun and events to look forward to. And we had a massive sports field and a couple of tennis courts. Two sports I have always loved and played. I played tennis with my best friend David and we also had a Spurgeon's football team, where we played other local teams from time to time. We weren't very good, but what we lacked in natural ability we made up for with passion and enthusiasm. Although matches against us could sometimes be a little violent, as we had a few tough nuts in our team, hardened by a lot of childhood fights. And if it was raining, indoors we had a games room, complete with record player and table tennis table. I would spend hours playing table tennis too.

And outside the grounds we had a magical coastline and beaches to explore on the Isle of Thanet. Birchington was so magical, with its chalk cliffs, caves and secret coves. And it extended onward to the beautiful and serene Minnis Bay – where a few of my good friends lived. So many happy and special times spent there.

Minnis Bay – Looking towards Reculver

And much time spent swimming and picnicking at the large expanse of Westgate-on-sea. And then a little way round the coast to the famous 'cockles and welks' resort of Margate itself; with a large sandy beach full of the sights and sounds of happy children, ice cream sellers, candy floss and pretty young girls everywhere! And all overlooked by the celebrated Margate sea front, with delicious odours from the seafront bars and cafes, of fresh cooked fish n' chips, of bingo callers ("on the red, big fat hen – number 10!") The buzz and sounds of the arcades - rock 'n roll music, pinball wizards and a myriad of different machines of every

conceivable type and vintage. And watching over it all, the magical sentinel of the scenic railway at the 'King of Funfairs' - **Dreamland** itself.
We also had the bonus of Ramsgate sea front, on schooldays in our lunch times. A beautiful harbour with the iconic Eagle Café, deep sandy beach and the appropriately named arcade - the Pleasurama.

Beautiful Ramsgate Beach and sea front – 1970's.
***Destined to live in a flat here, with my dream girl – 1980's.**

And inland from the homes was the green and glorious Kent Countryside – the Garden of England. I would so often venture off on my own, on my bicycle (called 'Silver'), exploring the nature, ecology, history and architecture of our frontline county. And also riding around the amazing Thanet coastline.
So there was endless fun to be had throughout the year, growing up in famous Kentish seaside resorts. Spurgeons had chosen their location well. 😊

Winters were freezing however, being on the North Kent coast. To this very day, I can still feel the chill of those winter mornings at Margate seafront, waiting for the bus; trying to shield from those vicious unforgiving North Easterlies, hitting your face with unrelenting stinging sleety rain. And as old school buildings tended to be chilly themselves, it could take all day to warm up – only to face it again on the way home in the dark. For those who've experienced an old-fashioned Thanet winter, will know that I exaggerate not how cold and bitter it was! It always snowed – every year. *Not complaining of course (I'm born and bred by the sea); I'm just trying to invoke the feel and vibe of those nostalgic distant days.*

But Spurgeons itself was a warm and cosy place and as well as our plays, Christmases were glowing and full of joy. Many children went back to relatives and 'blood' families at Christmas, but the children who stayed at the homes joined together in a visit from Santa, followed by a sumptuous communal feast, with lots of old-fashioned fun and games to follow.

I would then spend the rest of Christmas (sometimes with my brother Bill and a couple of other children, including David), with Uncle John at Brandon House.

I can still feel the glowing cordiality of those happy youthful festive days. Lovely presents, delicious food and drink, and extremely funny Christmas TV, often featuring "The Two Ronnies", "Morecambe and Wise", "Porridge", "Rising Damp" or the 'Monty Python's'.

The 70's was a most remarkable and memorable time for culture. Not only did we have fabulous and exciting pioneering bands and some of the great all-time classic movies, we also had timeless classics, such as "Monty Python", "The Sweeney" and "Star Trek". And brilliant musical movie gems of the day I loved – "Cabaret", "That'll be the Day" and "Stardust", and The Who's classic rock opera – "Tommy", featuring Elton John as the 'Pinball Wizard'.
Uncle John would also invite my Dad for supper and extend him hospitality, which I always truly appreciated, as I knew how lonely my Dad really was; so it was good to see him relaxed and feeling the warmth of a genuine welcome. 🤍

Christmas 1976 – Soccer 'hooligan' at the back!

1976 – 1978 - Rebellion

Having experienced such a wonderful Summer of 76, and feeling much more grown up, I began the 4th year seniors with a far more positive outlook and worked a lot harder than the previous year. I continued to go out with Deb, and Dad continued to visit at the weekends. But this was a new season of 1976 -77 and Arsenal had a new and progressive Irish manager – Terry Neill. And the club also bought us the gift of the new most expensive transfer in history to date – for £333,333 + 33p, we bought one Malcolm Macdonald (Supermac) from Newcastle, and with some very exciting young Irish players (O'Leary, Brady and Stapleton), the future looked bright, especially after the 2 previous seasons where we finished 16th and 17th respectively.
But most importantly, this was the season I joined the London branch of the Arsenal Supporter's club and started to go to the matches on my own. And at the same time, my schoolmates were doing the same – most of them following our rivals Chelsea, Spurs or Westham. But we'd get each other programmes and often travel together to London on the train, depending on who was playing at home or away. And as we got bigger and more ingrained as teenagers, we were essentially becoming trainee soccer hooligans. A state of affairs exacerbated by the release of a certain notorious single released on 26th November 1976 – one "Anarchy in the UK" by the Sex Pistols.

This was a seminal moment in not only musical and cultural history, but also in my own life. Here was something genuinely new and different. Here was change. Here was challenge. Here was the sound of rebellion! And there soon followed The Stranglers, The Damned and The Clash – with the late great Joe Strummer, who has been a major influence on my music and philosophy. *It is true to say that from this point on I was thinking I could really be in a band one day. After all, those guys had shown us that anyone could do it! But I didn't dare tell anyone my secret ambition. They'd only have laughed at me!* 🤣

As well as new bands, safety pins and spikey fashions, came the attitude to go with it. And myself and several of my mates were developing this in abundance, especially my football mates. Throughout 1977, as we grew in to young 'men', we became tougher and our bravado increased, and as well as attending many home games, I started to go to away games too. I loved the journeys, the freedom and the camaraderie. True, there were often scraps on the terraces, on the trains and at motorway cafes, but it was mostly testosterone driven 'tribal' nonsense! 🙄 I would get up really early in the morning and travel to London on my own. I preferred my independence and I could always hang out with the many Arsenal faces I met on my journeys. I travelled to games like Ipswich, Nottingham Forest, Manchester Utd and Wrexham – all over the place, and following the Arsenal became my first love.

Sadly, this meant that Deborah and myself didn't last beyond early 1977. She no doubt was fed up with my immaturity and increasingly 'bad' attitude. 🙄
That age gap really comes in to play at those ages. The football and punk would spill in to our school world and these would sometimes result in tribal team rivalry and fights. But I still got on with my work and achieved better results than the previous year and the teachers were generally happier with me.
That summer I also got my first proper holiday job at Regal Gifts, next to **Dreamland.** But it didn't last long, as I met 2 brothers called The Cains. They ran a fun but gimmicky 'hand writing analysis machine', which was placed in a booth on Margate seafront. Holiday makers would pay their money and sign a card which was fed in to the machine. And after strange noises and flashing lights, the machine would spit out a card telling them all their character traits, which I would interpret for them. 😉 The times I would hear "That's so accurate!" This position meant I was still getting closer to **Dreamland** and my destiny. I would now spend most of my holidays and half-terms at my friend Stevie B's home (with his lovely Mum – Joan, who would treat me as her own). And the rest of the breaks I was at Brandon House with Uncle John. And much to our delight, he took Bill and I and a couple of other boys to Lahnstein again that hot jubilee summer. We again, had a most magnificent and happy holiday. 🌞

At summer's end, as I had now reached 15 and was now officially 'a big boy', I believed more and more that I could do just what I liked! Alas, this meant that I became impossible for Barbara, so at the start of the 5th Year in September 1977, I was transferred to The

Lodge (formerly Sick Bay), but now just another house within Spurgeons, under the control of one Mr.B as my houseparent. The Lodge was a large building, all on ground level and near the back gates – making it much easier to sneak out at night! 😉 Mr.B didn't particularly like me from the start and to be honest the feeling was mutual. To be fair to him, I would imagine that I gave him quite a hard time; nevertheless, he didn't really have one good word to say about me. His first report on me from January 1978 starts with:-

Sept/Dec '77 John continues to live in a world entirely of his own, is extremely egotistical with apparently no thought for anything but Football. His paper-round now seems to be interfering with his punctuality at school where his progress would seem to be less than satisfactory. (see copy report) and he is currently insisting on leaving this summer although he openly admits that he has no idea whatsoever as to what he wants or could do in the 'world of work' and asserts that he has no ambition at all. His relationships with his father seems to be deteriorating if anything and John does not

His words read "John continues to live in a world entirely of his own, is extremely egotistical, (the right attributes for Lead Singer in a band! 😉) *with apparently no thought for anything but football. His paper round now seems to be interfering with his punctuality at school, where his progress seems to be less than satisfactory, and is currently insisting on leaving this summer, although he openly admits that he has no idea whatsoever as to what he wants or what he could do in the 'world of work'* (Lead Singer maybe? 🎤) *and asserts that he has no ambition at all.* (Other than to be a Lead Singer in a band! 😉) lol
His relationship with his Father seems to be deteriorating if anything ... etc. etc." (What's new?)
Tis' true that by now I was a gobby, rebellious, independent-minded 15-year-old 'punk', and my relationship with Dad was becoming strained at times. Now I was older, I wanted to visit the family home and stay over sometimes and see my old Dymchurch friends. I also believed I could be of practical help to him, as the house had been completely untouched since we left the place in such a hurry back in 74. Alas, he declined to allow me to visit essentially my own home, on the grounds that I wasn't practical like my younger brother and might 'burn the house down'! 😲 Dad's lack of foresight and sometimes complete oblivion to other's feelings (sometimes to the most insulting degree in my case), was often hard to take. I tried so hard to please him. More challenging still was

the constant playing my younger brother and I against one another. Bill was always so much more like him as a person, so they were much more compatible than he and I. And as we grew up, they grew closer, whilst my Dad and I struggled with one another. The problems finally came to a head one day in early 1978, when I told Dad to 'f*** off" over something. He moved towards me to give me a whack and I stood my ground – warning him that "If he hit me, I would hit him back!" He clearly knew I meant it, and so he backed off.
After this, he and I actually got on a lot better than we'd ever done, although I now spent a lot less time with him and my younger siblings, as I was often at football on Saturdays and had my own friends and life. But most importantly, asserting myself in that way had changed the dynamics completely and allowed me to feel far more confident in myself. I was growing up fast now! 💪
And after all, the punk revolution was here, and for me it symbolized freedom, possibility and potential. It actually changed my whole way of thinking and greatly enhanced my feeling that I needed to trust my own

heart. And when Sid Vicious released his visceral version of "My Way", this only served to channel my youthful rage, and accentuated my deep-seated determination that I really was going to do it MY WAY!

1978 – 1979 – Fostering and Work

By the end of January 78 (very soon after that report), poor old Mr.B had completely had enough of me, and I was transferred to another house temporarily with a houseparent I got on even worse with. And I couldn't stand it there. But suddenly everything changed. In the February, Spurgeon's cook Dorothy Fairbrother and her husband Ron offered to foster me. It would start as just weekends, and if it worked out, they would like to make it permanent. And by May, it was permanent and I was just sooo happy! I recall feeling the happiest that I'd been since Mummy had been alive. 😊
Uncle Ron and Auntie Dorothy lived in a beautiful detached house in Shakespeare Road, Birchington, with a large swimming pool. I had my own spacious bedroom, complete with its own sink and carpet tiles on the ceiling! I was treated like the son they never had and at first, was really spoiled. And I soon had a new girlfriend who I asked out at the Birchington Village centre (of course); my second St.George's girl – Mary, who was younger than me, but mature and developed for her age. She and her sister Carol (who was also a friend of mine) were both adopted and lived in Birchington with their parents. From the start, I was made very welcome in their home. Mary was charming and funny, but she was also very moody and often highly volatile and unpredictable. Nobody at her school or outside, not even the older girls (or boys for that

matter), would mess with her! But whilst I was more than a little scared of her myself, I admired those bold and brazen traits of hers. I saw it as strength. And she was always great fun! 👍

That early summer, I didn't do a lot of revision to be honest, but I completed my GCE's and did Ok, achieving 5 'O' levels. Although, at my school that wasn't considered a particularly outstanding success, it wasn't too bad at all, considering so much disruption in my secondary school years.

Spurgeon's Homes 1978 – Aged 16

I had a wonderful summer at the Fairbrother's, spending a lot of time with Mary around the poolside; listening loads to David Bowie, whom we both loved. ⚡ (particularly his 1977 classic "Low"), and all the great new sounds of 78, particularly the punk groups, with The Stranglers top of the bill. ♫

I decided to return to school in the autumn and join the 6th Form – repeat some 'O' levels and continue on to 'A' levels. But on my return, it was not the same at all. Many of my mates had left at the end of the 5th year to go to work, and school no longer felt like the right place for me. I was 'chomping at the bit' to get out in to the world and in to the work place. I could see no point in any further school education. I felt I could learn far more by getting out there. I applied for a job at a local factory, but the school were having none of it; they didn't want one of their pupils working in a factory! 😲 So they found me a job with the famous retailer at the time – Lipton's, who had shops all over the country at that time. My branch was at Westgate and I started in the second week of October 1978 for the tidy sum of £23 per week!

I enjoyed many aspects of working in a 'small' supermarket and was a 'natural' with the customers. I soon became very popular and by the end of November I was already being offered promotion, to join the Lipton's South-East merchandising team in the new year. This would mean travelling all over Kent,

Sussex and London refitting stores and organizing all the shelves, products and new lay-outs. And a pay rise! Meanwhile, my relationship with Mary was growing and we became very close. Auntie Dorothy was away a lot visiting her daughter in France, who had ongoing problems; so it was often just myself, Uncle Ron and Mary. They got on extremely well, to the point where I sometimes felt 'ganged' up on; but Mary was 'a blast' to be around and kept me 'right on my toes'. I would see my Dad and siblings occasionally, and my brother Bill would sometimes visit. But I had a new life now and I felt happier now than I had in years, with a real feeling of independence and some security. 😁
However, I had become accustomed to things not lasting, and on Dec 31st 1978 (New Year's Eve), I spilt up with Mary, after she went off with an older guy of about 18 years old – a soldier in the army. I mean, I couldn't exactly fight him! To be honest, I was absolutely inconsolable. I was totally obsessed with Mary, and although I realize now it wasn't true love in the sense I understand it now, at the time my world had fallen apart. 🥺
But I started my new job for Lipton's in the first week of January 1979 and was driven around in a Ford Capri by my immediate boss, one Robert F. I really warmed to him. He was firm, but easy-going and liked a drink and to smoke lots of cigarettes (as we all seemed to in those days! 🚬) As promised, we went all over the South-East to large, medium and small stores. I learned

so much and worked hard. I also loved the pub lunches we used to have most days. *Standard fare to drink at lunchtime in those days!* We also had large full weekend refits and merchandising on larger stores, where we were put up in hotels and B & B's. I loved being out and about, seeing different places, being creative with stock layout design and good solid company too, with an established reputation.
So much of my time was taken up with work now and I wasn't able to go to quite as many matches either. I had 2 great friends who lived in the station area of Birchington – Trevor J (who ran the sweet shop) and Phil T (who's Mum ran the Station Café). Trevor was almost 30, so a lot older than me. I saw him as a mentor. I would drink and smoke with him. He introduced me to poetry and also to Bob Dylan – which was life-changing for me. And we would go to the Lafayette night club in Birchington and clubs in Margate too, and get very 'smashed!' Phil was more sensible and would look after us both during these revelries.
But Trevor was also an excellent self-employed business man and I learned lots from him in this 'department'. And when the sweet shop was open and I wasn't at work for Lipton's, I would help Trevor in the shop. And sometimes a pretty young lady called Sue would come in after school; and soon we were going out together. Sue worked and lived in the famous Birchington Ice Cream Parlour right opposite.

Sue also went to St.George's School. We started going out with each other in the Feb 1979. In contrast to my last relationship, she was innocent, sweet and gentle. A little Pisces lady. A great listener - very bright, kind and compassionate. And she lived in the place that served the best **Knickerbocker Glorys** you would ever find! 😊 And we would stay up very late at her place above the shop, cuddled up, talking and listening to music. We particularly loved The Beatles, Genesis and the brand-new music sensation – Kate Bush. And for her birthday, I bought Sue tickets for Kate's famous Hammersmith Odeon show in the May, and we were right at the front. And then Kate Bush herself (who's family happened to live in Birchington), actually came in to the parlour the following month and signed Sue's programme. Sometimes Sue would come to my place, and we would again spend hours listening to music and talking. But I was far more possessive with her than any other girl I'd been out with, and I didn't want Uncle Ron interfering. Auntie Dorothy had still not come back from France and this was now proving challenging without a woman around. After all, it was her who had chosen to foster me. However, now I had a lovely new girlfriend, I was much happier. 😊

Also in the May of 1979, Arsenal finally won a trophy – the FA Cup; their first in the 8 years I'd been so loyally supporting them. We beat Man Utd 3-2 in the famous '5 minute' final. Alas, I wasn't able to get a ticket (even though I'd been to loads of games), so watched it at an

Arsenal mates. I was very happy and very drunk! 🤫
Sue put up with me and looked after me that night!

Triumphant Arsenal Team – May 1979

1979 was also the year I was reunited with my half-sisters after a 5-year estrangement, caused by my Father's sad intransigence. I had been pushing him for a long time to let us see our sister's again and he had finally relented, after my sister Wendy contacted him. I saw Wendy first, then my sister Rosie and then my sister Lissa, who had looked after us those 4 years after Mummy died. She was now married to Hugh – a Major in the British army and now had children of her own; so I would go to stay and spend time with my new niece and nephew. I got on very well with my little baby nephew Luke *(a strong bond that has stood the test of time).* 💜

Reunited with sister Wendy - 1979

My sister Wendy was a nurse who lived in Rayner's Lane London; and I would stay at her place, which was also my London base for the Arsenal. I always got on very well with her. She was easy going, didn't care how much I drank or smoked, and just let me be myself. She also had (and has always had), a 'wicked' sense of humour. She also lived near our beloved Auntie Peggy – so I got to spend time with her and her family again. And then finally, I got to see my eldest sister Angeline. There was also a new Prime Minister, one Margaret Thatcher. And even though I instinctively disliked her, she was a 'sweeping new broom'. So it really did seem like this was maybe a fresh new time for the forthcoming Eighties and that things might be looking up for officially the last year of my childhood! However, like all 'self-fulfilling prophecies', it didn't last. And it altered most suddenly. By my 17th birthday, my work situation had completely changed, Trevor had suddenly gone abroad, my foster-home and relationship with Uncle Ron broke down, and worst of all, I'd split up with Sue.

There was no real reason for this to happen, as we seemed to have a strong bond and got on well, other than perhaps I drank and smoked too much! But I did kinda' talk myself out of going out with her, and she just unexpectedly ended it one evening. I remember being almost ambivalent at the time – like I expected it and didn't really care; but there is no doubt looking back that I was deeply affected. **I didn't see or hear from Sue again for 30 years, until we found each other again on "Friend's Reunited". Curious how she'd looked for me first and I for her first, and then the website closed soon afterwards. We began writing and I am delighted to say that she has become a dear and trusted friend for many years now. I knew we had some kind of bond. And with the way our lives turned out, we both now know the real reason we parted all those years ago. We both had other destinies to fulfil!*

My foster home had mainly 'broken down' because Auntie Dorothy wasn't around much, due to the problems with her daughter abroad. I started to argue lots with Uncle Ron over all kinds of things. Why I didn't bring Sue home more and because I would roll

up in the early hours from Sue's. He also didn't like the music I played, particularly "No More Heroes", nor my argumentative, strong-willed attitude.
At work, my boss Robert's two little girls were tragically run-over and killed up at Joss Bay, whilst the family were just out enjoying themselves one Sunday afternoon. 🥲 I recall having trouble assimilating this information. How could such terrible 'random' things like this happen? ☹ What it meant for me was the cessation of us travelling around together doing merchandising, as he was granted extended leave. So I was sent to different stores for weeks or fortnights to work with the management of those stores. I travelled by train and they paid all my expenses. I enjoyed this time on my own travelling around Kent.
My social worker also found me 'digs'. A tiny room in a terraced house with a husband-and-wife Brian and Janet G (with baby) in Cross Road, Birchington. They were a decent working-class couple and I got on well with them. But I was out most of the time anyway. In my spare time I would get 'smashed' and my mate Phil would have to look after me. I was also now developing a serious gambling habit. Before it had only been fruit machines. Now I was old enough to get in to the bookies (not officially but I could get away with it), it was the horses and dogs and I would lose lots. 😰 And as with any gambling addiction, I would 'chase' until finally I lost all my money. Let me make this absolutely clear – gambling addiction is a frightening

and soul-destroying place to be. It's almost impossible to describe the turmoil and inner feelings of hopelessness, but it IS an illness.

**Nowadays, we see an almost endless stream of gambling ads, accompanied by the slogan "Gamble responsibly". Yeah – easier said than done if you're an addict. The people who invented that slogan (probably the government or one of their agencies), have absolutely no understanding of how gambling addiction works. Nobody wants to gamble irresponsibly. The word 'responsible' is hardly synonymous with an almost uncontrollable addiction. When you're in that state, you just keep gambling. You are not in a sane mental state. One is unwell.*
Trust me I know – sheer misery.

**I am happy to report that these days, I can have a fun bet a couple of times a year – on The Derby and The National, without any addictive feelings whatsoever. d.v*

"It ain't my fault it's six 'o'clock in the morning"
He said - As he came up out of the night.
When he found I had no coins to bum, he began to testify
Born in a depression, born out of good luck, born into misery ..
In the back of a truck.
I'm telling you this mister, don't be put off by looks.
I been in the ring and I took those right hooks.
Oh the loneliness used to knock me out - harder than the rest.
And I've worked for breakfast, and I ain't had no lunch
I been on delivery and received every punch."

The Clash – Broadway

1980 - 1st Half – 'Broadway' – Part 1

So by the end of 1979, I was heavily drinking, gambling and smoking and I'd become unsettled, depressed and unhappy. ☹ Brian had talked me in to coming to work at Haffenden's (a hot water bottle factory where he worked), for double the money that Lipton's were paying me. So I impetuously left them and went to work humping boxes at the factory. It was actually horrible. There was nowhere grimmer than the Sandwich Industrial Estate at 5am on a freezing January morning. I was 'going nowhere' and it only lasted a month. I got a job as a trainee manager at the new Co-Op hypermarket in Westwood – again, only lasting a month. Whilst at the store, I had met one Alan BL in the foyer. He was actually selling cavity wall insulation for a company called Warmawall. Coincidently, (*although I don't believe in that word),* Alan and his family had taken over Trevor's sweet shop in Birchington. So in early 1980, I left Co-Op and went to work as a 17-year-old door-to-door salesman (without a car), working commission only for Warmawall. And even though I was way too young to be a salesman, I found I had an aptitude for it. I did get a couple of sales 'under my belt', but obviously such a precarious situation couldn't last.

I would occasionally earn a little extra income by working for Alan at the sweet shop (now called 'Sweet Talk'), but this was limited. Sue never came in either. And I found myself missing her lots. ☹ I would try to supplement my income with gambling and this now extended to the casino at Ramsgate, where I could get in with Alan. I didn't see my Dad very much and considered he had no real power over me now anyway. I had the same attitude with my social worker. By the early spring, I was starting to get a little behind with my rent and my drinking, smoking and gambling were out of control. I would get so drunk I would just lay in the middle of the road and not even know where I was or even who I was – by now, I was lost. 😦

Poor old Phil would have to literally drag me home at times. In early spring '80, Alan decided to expand his 'empire' and discussed with me about opening Margate's first sex shop, to be called "Pillow Talk" – and I would be helping him set it up and working in there. And whilst I felt all grown-up and seizing an opportunity, this was hardly a promising, nor particularly healthy option for a naive young man still officially in care. I went along with it, but felt awkward and out of my depth.

My big escape was still the Arsenal and I went to several matches that season, which culminated in us getting to the Cup Final again in May – this time against second division Westham. And I wasn't intending to miss out on attending this time. But I had no ticket and not enough money. And so true to form, I went to the bookies with my earnings (including the rent) and inevitably lost. This was the 'final straw'. I borrowed some money from a friend, and without telling a soul where I was going, I 'did a runner' on the day of the final, taking an Arsenal mate with me. I bought a ticket from a tout and we infamously lost 1-0. I left Wembley in tears that day, without a clue where to go next. So inspired by my favourite film of the time "That'll be the Day", I ended up down in Brighton. I got a job selling ice creams on the beach – lasted a day. I imagined staying there and somehow getting in a band. I slept on the beach and then at a B & B. Watched Arsenal lose the European Cup Winners Cup Final – losing 5-4 on penalties to Valencia in Brussels. Felt like a real loser. I also ran out of money again, so I hitch-hiked up the country and ended up in Bedford with Barbara again, and my two younger siblings Lizzie and Eddie. Only then did my Dad and the social services discover that I was actually 'safe and well'. **After Spurgeon's Homes in Birchington closed, the emphasis was on fostering. But this was not always possible or successful, so Spurgeons set up new smaller self-contained houses in the Midlands in places like Luton, Coventry and Bedford. And my 2 younger siblings found themselves (via a disastrous and abusive fostering placement) in Bedford, back with Barbara. My brother Bill was the last in the homes and eventually found a placement in Birchington.*

Barbara let me stay for a few days, whilst it was discussed what was to become of me – now a nearly 18 year's old jobless, 'n'er do well', runaway, gambling, drinking and smoking soccer 'hooligan' – soon to be officially out of care. 🙄
My sister Lissa and her husband Major Hugh, kindly offered to let me come and stay with them in their army home in Bicester, Oxfordshire. So I spent the early part of the summer there, and got a job in a local tailors ("suit you sir!"😉) And although I continued to smoke a lot of fags, I was able to get my drinking and gambling under control (at least for a time). My sister insisted on clean living! 🖖
I had really loved staying with Lissa and Hugh since our reconciliation the year before, but living there was another matter. My sister was loving and kind like she'd always been, but I found Hugh difficult, a tad too judgemental, and way too regimental for a free spirit like me. No doubt I must have seemed like a real 'pain' to him, as his wife's wayward and unruly younger brother; and it was fairly obvious that he didn't like me very much. We would incessantly argue.**I am pleased to say that in later years we became very good friends and he became a true brother and advocate for me; so I actually ended up liking and respecting him immensely.* But back in 1980 – it was no fun at all.
And as I'd done 'a runner' a couple of months before, all my stuff was in storage at my Dad's. So I literally only had one tape to listen to during those early

summer weeks - “ABBA’S Greatest Hits 2” – which I played over and over. What fantastic music! 🎹 What a glorious sound! 🎶 I would put on headphones, close my eyes and let the gorgeous music take me. The song “Eagle” would send me off to special dreamscapes full of joy and romance. And to realms where my own ABBA girl might exist!
But all in all, in these last days of my childhood, I felt lonely and lost. ☹ I desperately needed a way out. In fact, I needed a miracle!

“Singing songs with lungs of fire, right on to the wire ...
Storm that bought you to my shore, ripping rapping on your door ... On your door, like a claw.
The olde sage takes a bow, do you see the clock on steeple high – it’s chiming! Miracles!
It’s chiming...miracles. It’s chiming...miracles.”

Jayl - “Chiming (Miracles) 🕛 ***© 2002***

“A beach is a place where a man can feel
He's the only soul in the world that's real”

Pete Townshend – THE WHO – “Bell Boy”

1980 – 2nd Half – 'Broadway' – Part 2

On the morning of June 27th 1980, Dad suddenly died of a brain haemorrhage. He was working beneath one of his Morris Minors at the time. It would have been almost instantaneous, so he wouldn't have suffered. By the evening, I was at the William Harvey Hospital in Ashford, Kent, where I met my brother Bill. I had to break the sad news to him and he was inconsolable. He and Dad had been very close. I then witnessed Dad laying peacefully at rest. It's the first time I'd ever seen anyone dead before. It was very strange, yet somehow comforting. I was able to say goodbye to my Dad without him answering back, and with some forgiveness in my heart. I was relieved that he'd had a quick and painless end and I was also elated that he'd 'chosen' this moment to depart from us. It was literally 35 days to my 18th birthday. **So now, I really was a full orphan**. I spent the night at the hospital and swear I heard my Dad calling me. It was so lucid, it was more than a dream.**After many years deliberation, I believe I know what he was trying to tell me. RIP old fellow.* †
I awoke the next morning to the most glorious summer's day. The birds were heartily singing and the sky was blue. I left the hospital and whilst I was sad about my Dad, I felt such an exhilarating sense of freedom, I can feel the emotions to this very day. I called my social worker and he collected me and took me down to "Runnymede" – the family home in

Dymchurch – for which I now had the keys. I felt grown-up and that I was now the ‘man of the family’ and also the ‘king of the castle’. And so almost 6 years to the day since we’d so hurriedly left – I was home and I was free. My Dad had actually written me a ‘final’ letter, although of course he didn’t know this. It lay on the table, with a stamp, ready for posting. Alas, his last words to me (*aside from “Love Dad”*), were that “music and salesmanship will get you nowhere.” A rather unfortunate and insensitive prophecy for that moment. 🥲 So after reading those words, which at the time wounded me deeply, I worked very hard in life to make sure that I prove that misguided ‘prophecy’ entirely wrong. *My Dad was an old school, get a proper job, stick to it and never have a day off kind of guy. He actually wanted me to join the army. And with the benefit of hindsight, I absolutely respect his motivations and those kind of conventional values.* But alas, for a totally free, rebellious and wild spirit like myself, who just wanted to front a rock n’ roll punk band and show off; those ideas were just anathema to me. 🎸 I lived at my social worker’s for 3 weeks, and then moved in to “Runnymede”, back by the seaside and the beach, just in time for my 18th Birthday. 👑 The welcome I received from my Dymchurch friends was as if I’d never left. *One of them told me that after I disappeared in 1974 and none of them knew where I’d gone, that they’d kept a chair open for me, in case I ever returned.* And they were true to their promise. 😊

**To this day I am invited to all the Southland's School, New Romney, Class of 78 leavers events, even though I only spent one year there, in the first-year seniors. So this is a genuine honour for me. And I realized on my return how special I was to all my Dymchurch friends. And we still see each other and we're still all the same really. Just older, larger versions of what we were then. After all, we've known each other since we were 5!*

With my dear friend Jacqui P
Final Runnymede Party – November 1980
Phil T in the background

"Suddenly I noticed that it weren't quite the same
Felt different one morning, maybe it was the rain."

The Clash – Broadway

Romney Marsh Summer (and a final party!)

That summer I celebrated my 18th birthday. I felt generally happy and finally free. But it was a huge task to sort out the house and my Dad's estate, especially for one so inexperienced. Moreover, 2 weeks after my Dad passed away, my Dad's elderly Aunt, (my Great Aunt Gladys) passed away in a nursing home. I did visit her just the once. She was drifting in and out of sleep and didn't know who I was. It was so sad. And as I was her eldest surviving relative, I had to deal with her funeral, house and estate as well. Nevertheless, it was truly moving and enlightening going through the archives and diaries of their lives.
It was also intensely profound to return to my childhood home to find most of the house and my bedroom untouched, and exactly as I left it so hurriedly, 6 years before. My Dad had literally only used 3 rooms and all that had been added to my bedroom were layers and layers of dust. On my first visit, I stood in its telling silence in deep and reflective contemplation. When I'd left, I was a little boy, now I was a young man.
I spent loads of time with my friends that summer, especially in the ancient old locals of Dymchurch and the Romney Marsh. And David M would visit too, We held a funeral for my Dad, which all my 7 siblings attended. Actually the penultimate time we would all be together. We also had a funeral for my Great Aunt,

with only myself and her 2 last friends in attendance. It was a most sad and poignant event. 😔
So here I was now almost 18, with no 'blood' parents, grandparents, aunties or uncles left in my life. I really was now the 'man' of the family and assumed the role to the best of my ability. And my new found freedom gave me the chance to express myself and plan a new future. So I started writing songs again. 🎼 Well actually the poetry and lyrics part to start with. **The first I'd written since I was a little boy at Dymchurch Primary, where I'd introduced lunch time 'Top of the Pops.'*
But because I hadn't kept up the art through my troubled teenage years, I'd literally forgotten how to write. But re-inspired by particularly Bob Dylan and The Beatles, those first few tentative writings started to take shape. So ready to join my first band then! 🎤
I spent my 18th with my sister Wendy, hanging out in London. She bought me the new Peter Gabriel album – "Gabriel 3" – a seminal masterpiece, which has influenced me greatly. *#GamesWithoutFrontiers* 🎶
And most providentially, on Aug 27th I answered an ad in New Romney for a local band looking for a singer. Turned out to be a guy called Jeremy P, who was actually a cousin of Gabriel! 😲 I attended a couple of rehearsals in a huge barn out at Ivychurch, but didn't really have a clue what I was doing, or how to sing songs like "Alright Now" by Free. 😉
I did get a job at Sainsbury's for September as a trainee manager; a good job to be honest, with prospects; but

in my heart I only had one objective – to be a lead singer/songwriter in a great band. So I set my heart on this and ended my short career in retail. I bought myself my first motorbike (a Honda CB 100) and came off in the first week round the twisty roads at Burmarsh. Lucky my best mate Will G was with me to rescue my bike from the edge of the dyke, whilst his dear Mum cleaned and patched me up. It was a valuable lesson, as I learned to ride properly after that, and was much more careful. I found it exhilarating to ride around the Romney Marsh and beyond. I loved the wind in my face and the sense of freedom and constantly moving forward fast. This has always defined my very nature. That summer/early autumn I also made-up lost time by riding the line on one of the magnificent steam trains of my beloved Romney, Hythe and Dymchurch Railway – my most favourite place on the planet. 🚂 And I re-bonded with so many of my first friends who had remained so loyal; names all special to me (and almost without exception, friends to this very day). Will G, Andrew F, Brian B, Lola Jane, Tina S, Jacqui P, Sue B, Philip O, Phil M, Keith T, Andy O, Frances G, Sandra L, Kevin B, Graham C, Dougie. My confidence grew stronger that summer and I was feeling ready for adult life. 😊 I was also fortunate in that my next door neighbour – one Sue L, and her lovely daughter Lucy, would continually check on me, offer practical help, and 'spoil' me too.

In October, I received a letter from the solicitors of my late Father's estate, telling me I needed to vacate the house as it was now being put up for sale, along with a piece of land opposite, proceeds to be divided between the 8 of us. I felt most dismayed by this, as property and land prices were particularly low at that time, so I didn't feel the process should be rushed. Moreover, I actually wanted to keep the land, as I knew it would become valuable at a later date. Furthermore, this was now my home and after a childhood spent mostly in care, I didn't have anywhere else to go. Nevertheless, I was 'outvoted' by my older sisters, so had no choice but to pack up. 🙄
But like so many things that have happened in my life, this was a massive 'blessing in disguise'.🖖 d.v
I finished sorting the house and packed and made arrangements for the rest of the stuff in the house to go to my sister's place until we could all meet up and divide everything fairly. (*Alas, this never actually happened for me.*)
I made plans to move back to Birchington and stay at my brother Bill's foster home, with his foster-parent Pam and her sons. It was a small terraced house so there wasn't a lot of room, so I would only have the settee to kip on. But Pam kindly said she was prepared to let me do this until I found my own bedsit. My old scout master Bryan Southern (who ran a double-glazing company) offered me a job as a commission only window salesman and also proposed to teach me

'direct sales' properly (which he did). But most importantly of all, I talked my way in to joining my brother's first band "The Spirals", as the lead singer. Happy days! 🎤
So with all this pending, on Saturday Nov 1st, we held a big fat farewell party at "Runnymede", which had been dusty and neglected for too long. So for one last night, the old house came alive again, and was buzzing like it used to be back in the day when I was a little child; at those wonderful happy parties at Christmas and on birthdays, back when Mummy was alive.
The girls cleaned and dusted the house as much as they could and put up the 'family' decorations. We lit the old gas lamps and lots of candles and I prepared the music for the night. We acquired a large quantity of booze, cigarettes and snack food and my man arrived with quality herbs! 🚬 🍺 🍾
And that night not only did David come down, plus most of my Dymchurch friends; but almost all the young people from the village of that era passed by at some stage of the night! 😉
It was an awesome event, and we partied all night!

And even though many were 'worse for wear', there was no trouble. It was a joyous and happy occasion and the perfect culmination of my childhood and proper send off for my adult journey. 👍
The next day all was quiet again. There was only David and myself left, with the echoes of music and party fun still ringing in our ears, and feeling 'more than a little' hung over! I saw him to his bus in to the village. The weather had turned and it was absolutely freezing. I saw a girl's shoe on the pavement in Dymchurch. Later I found out it was my dear friend Lola Jane's and she'd somehow lost it! 👠 Oh those days of dizzy-headed youth. I smiled a very big smile – what a send-off we'd given the old house, and what a send-off for little 'ole me! Not so little now! 😉
Two days later, I packed up my final things and locked up the family home for the last time. That evening, I arrived back in Birchington and officially joined the band – The Spirals. My new life had begun. **I'm** the lead singer now and I'm going to be **Jayl** 🎤

You could say "I can see the Light! Roll! Forward! Drive! Green Lights! Green Lights! I Can See the Light!"
The Clash – Broadway

Friday November 7th 1980 – Serendipity *by Jayl* Birchington Village Centre *(Revisited)*

Exactly 6 years to the day after that a 12-year-old boy went to his first disco, at the Birchington Village Centre, he returned to the same venue as an 18-year-old young man, for one last under-18 disco! Many adventures had passed and he had been out of social services care for 3 months now. And he'd joined his first band that very week. So as the lead singer, he didn't want to turn up at the first rehearsal without a girlfriend. 😉 So he went to the disco. At 8.20pm (yes 20-20 vision), he spotted on the dance floor the most beautiful girl he'd ever seen – one Nikola Glass from Margate (Niki) And for him it was love at first sight. ♥

Niki Glass – 1980

And he plucked up the courage to ask her to dance. And she said **"yes!"**

And she was an orphan too (lost her Dad at 7 like he had lost his Mum at 7). And he asked her out. And she said **"yes!"** And he got to kiss her at the end of the evening. ❤ And then he went home and told his band he'd just met the girl he was going to marry! (Not that she knew that! 😉) *Serendipity*

And the next night he took her on a first date to see "The Blues Brothers." *Cool right?!* And he walked her home. And the next day he invited himself round to her house (always bold!) And on the Monday, he arrived at her cosy little home on his motorbike – smart, sharp, smelling great and bang on time! And waiting for him with such a warm welcome were his beautiful new girlfriend Niki, and her wonderful, kind and caring Mum – Betty. And they took him in and fed him, stray cat that he was! And as he'd been taught, he displayed impeccable manners and charm. And he and Betty got on very well. And she invited him back the next night, and then the next. *You know what strays are like!* 🐈

And after this, he was there most evenings. And she became his second Mum. And then her sister - Niki's Auntie Evelyn, and her husband Frank, invited him round to their lovely home. And with most splendid hospitality, treated him like he was one of the family too. *He also became friends with Niki's younger cousin (also called John). He was a pianist and they would eventually end up in a band together, writing songs.*

John and Niki hung out loads in Margate. They would go to the beach and the arcades and drink at the harbour at the famous Bar Majestic. And they'd often visit the Wimpy and tuck in to a delicious **Knickerbocker Glory** each! And most of all, they would go to **Dreamland** and ride the scenic railway, the big wheel and kiss and cuddle in the river caves. And these were the days when there were no selfies. Young lovers would always use the passport photo booths. And then John actually got a job in a sea front booth and then also at **Dreamland** itself (just inside the entrance), *as the Cain brothers now had 2 'handwriting analysis' machines on Margate front.* Happy Days indeed! 😊

So John and Niki did proper old-fashioned courting and were inseparable. And they fell madly in love. And then they got married. And they both loved cats. And steam trains. And great music. And concerts, And **ABBA**! 🌟

And David Bowie. *And of course – he introduced her to the **Arsenal**, and she fell in love again, eventually becoming Niki Gunner.* And they built an incredible life together which has stood the test of time.
Oh, and guess what? Many have said over the years that Niki looks a lot like beautiful Frida from ABBA! That's right, dreams really do come true! ♥

Margate Beach – December 1981

Mum – Hythe Station
RHDR - 1981

Glorious Day! August 25th 1984

My stunning and beautiful bride! ❤

Knickerbocker glory! An orphan's story –
Becomes a **love** story ❤
And so a **love** story …
And **my** story … Become **our** story.
Told through the decades – in photographs
and film. Through poetry, rhyme and song …

And so John and Nikola become **Jayl & Niki** **(another story)**,
and as they say, the rest is history…

And 42 years on ….. 😊❤

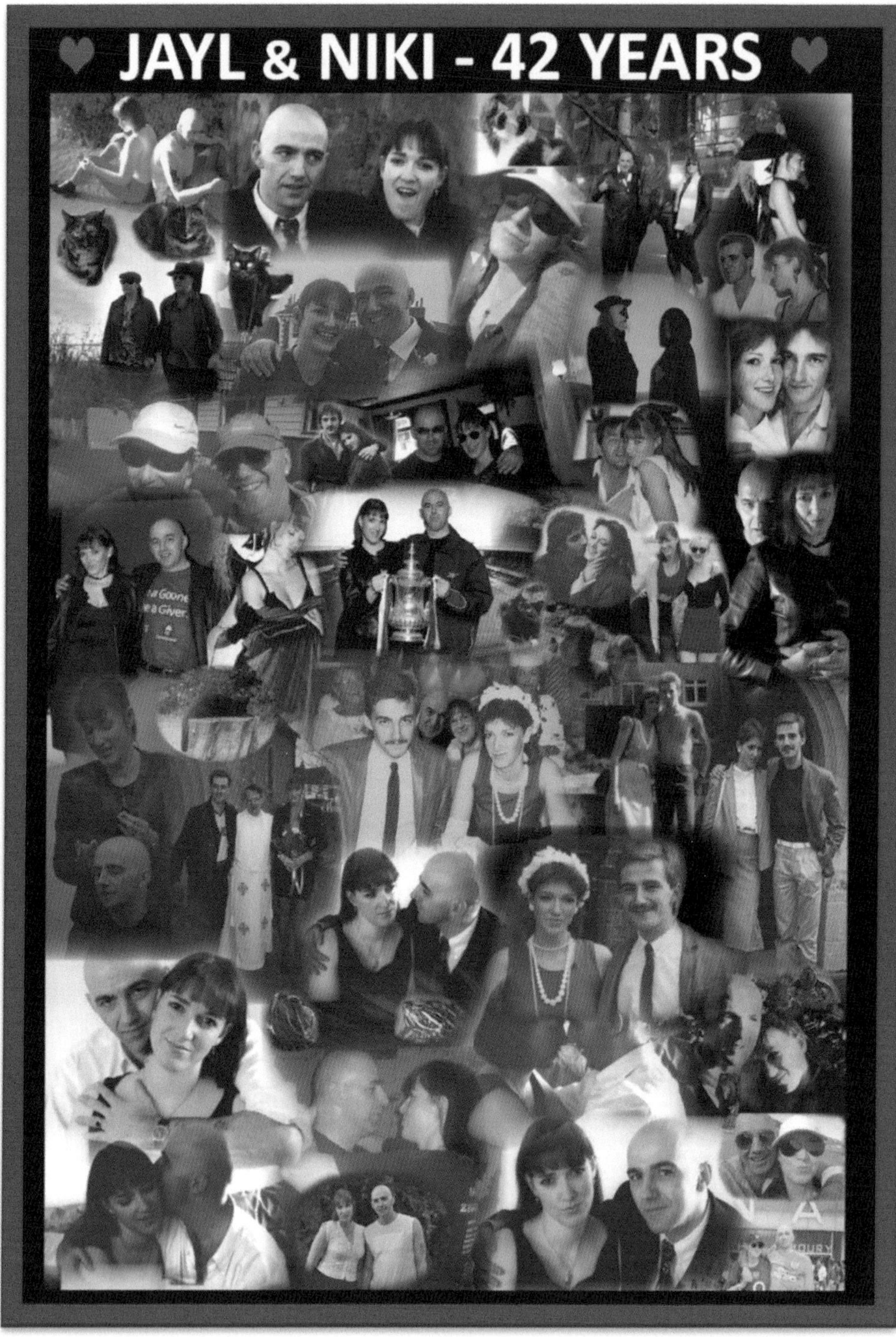
JAYL & NIKI - 42 YEARS

POSTSCRIPT 1: - FW > May 26th 2022 – LONDON ABBA VOYAGE – *by Jayl*

I stood amazed! On the floor of the fantastic newly constructed **ABBA ARENA.** It is **ABBA Voyage** - Opening Night. World Premiere. Mesmerized, hypnotized and over the moon. 🌛
How far had I come since that lonely and uncertain Summer of 1980, when I used to sit on my own listening to "Eagle" and dreaming of my own beautiful ABBA girl?!? And now all these years later here she was in front of me, my hands holding her shapely hips as she moved rhythmically to the music. My very own "Dancing Queen!" And my face next to the back of her hair, which had an aroma like hazelnut coffee. And combined with her fresh and summery 'Green Tea' perfume, made me feel heady and exhilarated – a beautiful natural drug! And I felt so proud to be here with her at this stage in our lives – after all this time still her loyal man, but now so much more. Her personal head of security for one thing. And what an honour and a privilege to be invited to the world premiere of ABBA VOYAGE, as chauffeur and minder to Niki, and as one of only 1,000 fans invited by the ABBA international fan club. Reserved for only their most loyal of their fans.
And sitting just behind us were **ABBA** themselves, watching their own avatars on stage, utilizing the most pioneering 21st Century technology, where the moves of the avatars were performed in advance by the band

themselves. And after this timely and intense process, meticulously digitized to create a version of reality where if you have the knowledge and the imagination, you really can be **any age in any time**.
And the girls' vocals were as harmonious and sonorous as ever, with delightful new songs like "Ode to Freedom", "Don't Shut me Down" and "I Still Have Faith in You" – as impeccable Ulvaeus/Andersson compositions as you could ever wish to hear. As good as anything from the past. And to all of this magnificence, ABBA added a fantastic and vibrant new young backing band! Ageless, visionary, pioneering and timeless magic! **And here I was at the centre of it.** With this beautiful hot lady of my life! And with the most incredible 360-degree soundscape and lightscape of perfection. And then "Eagle" is performed. And I think maybe "I've died and gone to heaven!" 😉
And with Frida and Agnetha's voices sounding as great as ever they have done; and in some ways even better – with a slightly bassy edge, forged over many years, with their long-life wisdom and vast experience of the joys and sorrows of life. And the incredible musical production of Benny Andersson and Björn Ulvaeus just awe-inspiring and meticulous. So much ahead of its time – absolute genius! And this timeless music combined with stunning and unbelievable visuals throughout, and the massively complex creation of the avatars directed and produced by Benny's son – Ludvig Andersson.

Thus bewildered and breathless we soak it all in with childlike wonderment. The band are performing on stage and it is ABBA - circa:1977.
And their avatars are coming out of the ceiling towards us sooo close up and in your face!
And at the same time the band ABBA – 2022, are sitting behind us exactly as they are now! 😮

And in some parts of the show the ABBA avatars are wearing most futuristic costumes. It is like the timeline itself has been conquered! And now at this point in the show "Eagle" is playing; accompanied by a mysterious and hypnotic video animation, with a Swedish snowy forest scape filling the huge stage screen - its stunning and dazzling visuals of dancing light and snowflakes leaking in to the circled mirror ceiling of the arena, escaping the mere confines of a 2-dimensional screen - showering us like sparkly snow and immersing us in a kaleidoscope of light and sound and vision. ☆

The feeling for me was of musical healing and harmony from a wondrous and magical multi-dimensional other realm, that seemed to touch and cleanse one's very soul. I stood in wonderment and awe, tears of sheer emotion, joy and happiness streaming down my face! (Many tears shed this night). And it felt like I'd come full circle. All the way round. And such a long way...

"Flying high, high, I'm a bird in the sky (I'm an eagle)
I'm an eagle that rides on the breeze
High, high, what a feeling to fly (what a feeling)
Over mountains and forests and seas
And to go anywhere that I please."

Benny Andersson / Björn Ulvaeus © Polar Music

#ABBAVOYAGE

POSTSCRIPT 2: FW > June 18th 2022 – MINNIS BAY - BIRCHINGTON – SPURGEON'S REUNION

Just 3 weeks later; and still feeling the euphoria of the ABBA Voyage Premiere, I found myself responding to another most special and auspicious invitation. Twas a most beautiful sunny breezy summer Saturday afternoon - I drove over to Kearns Hall in Minnis Bay, Birchington, for my first ever Spurgeon's Reunion. And I'd also been asked to deliver a speech for the occasion.
Most importantly, I would be meeting Auntie Barbara again, for the first time in over 40 years! I was therefore most grateful that my old best friend David M would also be there, and would also be speaking.

The day was very special and truly remarkable. Such a magical afternoon. Not only did I get to see Barbara again (and got on famously with her), I also got to see my old housemate Susan B, who was there with her wonderful husband. We all sat at the same table for tea like a little family, just like we had all those years ago back in Stockwell House. It was an emotional afternoon. Many tears were shed; especially for Susan's younger sister Karen, who so sadly, had recently passed away after serious illness.
I remembered Karen's lovely smiling face back in the day. Everyone had their story and every story was tough, emotional, and very moving; but also filled with such acceptance and gratitude.

My friend David (who at 16 years was actually the child who was in the homes the longest), stood up and delivered a most powerful and poignant speech. One thing that really shone out from his words is that Spurgeon's had kept us safe. That many children of those times fell prey to sinister characters in state run homes. And that we had indeed been most fortunate and blessed. 😇 The underlying theme was of a group of faithful people, all united by being Spurgeon's children, refusing to harbour any bitterness or resentment - only great thankfulness and joy that we were safe, loved and cared for so well – and that by the grace of God, had survived our childhoods and lived to see this day.

And whatever our ages, or whatever era of the homes we were from, or how long we were there , we all felt like one big family. We sung the special old Spurgeon's hymn at the end - "Sequimini Optima" ("Try for the best") - *a motto I hold close to me and have always strived to live by. *And by trying for the best – I've often found the best!* 😊

So it was with a full heart of gratitude and joy that I was able to deliver my speech and personally thank Barbara for all she did for me, and putting up with me at such a difficult phase of my development.

Moreover, to engage in some banter by reading out some of the comments on those old blue report cards. This certainly raised a few laughs, mainly at my own

expense rather than Barbara's. And to be fair, she was very moved and kindly told me so afterward.
Most of all, I spoke of faith and destiny, and of miracles and powers beyond ourselves.
So I shared the story of that auspicious first night in Spurgeons and Barbara encouraging me to go to that first Birchington Village Centre Disco on Nov 8th 1974, as a young boy. And how I returned to that very place, on Nov 7th 1980 (almost exactly 6 years later) as a young man, to meet the girl of my dreams. A true tale of life and love and serendipity.

With Auntie Barbara and my Housemate Susan B
Spurgeon's Reunion – Minnis Bay – June 18th 2022

POSTSCRIPT 3: - MAN OF THE SUN 🌞
by Jayl & The Band of Life

Before in the age of time – when the man of the sun came by …
Weather-beaten and many times crushed - But we're gonna tell his story – so hush!
From the crossroads he came where the devil was smart - Bought his sword and his soul and his bleeding heart …

But the Lord he was abidin' on the dusty old track,
He knew right away he was under attack.
Came out from the rocks – he was all dressed in black.
Drew a picture in the air and that was that.
He offered salvation and bought the man back …
And freed him from the curses and the spells and the rack.
And then – it was the age of the gun – twas time for the man of the sun … To find love in the midst of the mire,
Whilst living on the edge of the wire.
Heard all of the bluff and excuses before …

From sorcerers and witches behind bloody red doors …
But in the desert beneath the giant blue skies,
In the blistering domain of the lord of the flies.
Through the hot-haze shimmer he heard the vulture's cries,
By the scorpions and sand, he stared the eagle in the eyes.
In defiance he challenged the fakeness and the lies,
Neath the ancient mountains, the warriors rise.

Then followed the age of the moon – the man of the sun hummed a tune …
With his guitar, his girl and his songs,
And the passion to right a few wrongs.
But on the plains of oblivion he saw that old devil fall,
Saw the kingdom rising and the breaking of the wall.
He danced in to the night with the girl of his desire,
Watching stars fall from heaven and the angels of fire.

And now the time it has passed – like a comet it was speeding too fast …
But redemption's the name of the game,
And for the faithful, no lingering pain.
And all's become timeless and stardust on the ground,
You cannot hear a whisper; you cannot hear a sound …
The silence is deafening, but not for the cats,
And all eyes are healed and freed from the rats.
Their enemies in terror with nowhere to run,
Wishing they could go back and make it undone,
Now the girl she just smiles, for the sorrow is done,
As she walks hand in hand with the man of the sun.

Such sadness for the days that were shattered,
By the madness and nothing that mattered …
Now they stand their ground, they'll not be bullied or battered ….Oh no!
As the man of the sun sings his song.
"Ooh Ooooh, Ooh Ooooh, Ooh Ooooh!"

Lyrics by Jayl
Music by Jayl / Booth-Spain
From the "Man of the Sun" EP

Pegwell Bay with my Niki – MAN OF THE SUN – 2019 🌞

And Finally … "QUEEN OF SPRING"

Healing from childhood trauma can take a lifetime. But the truth can set you free. It took a long time, but now I only feel gratitude and happiness for my childhood and for my life.

My hope in writing this memoir is not only to tell my story whilst bringing healing to myself, but also to bring inspiration and healing to my students, friends and relatives, or just anyone who may need a helping hand or a kind word. For I would never say "I am healed"; I will only say "By the Lord's grace I am healed." For there is another saying - "But for the Grace of God, go I" – which is a spiritual way of expressing how different things might have been, should events have taken a slightly different turn. 🙏 Another way of acknowledging how fortunate one has been, and to give credence and thanks to powers and forces other than ourselves. For this is the source of true healing. And this healing can only be fully accomplished through acceptance, forgiveness and faith. I didn't have long with Mummy; but her teaching underpinned all that I am today and provided me with the grounding that I would need to survive in an often-harsh world. I was privileged and blessed to have that time, however short. Nevertheless, it was over 50 years before I could finally write about Mummy with an open heart; in full acceptance and joy, and with gratitude and unconditional love. ❤

So I made it in to a poem – and then a song! ♫

I say "Hey, hello again ... I say "Hey, hello again ...

Queen of Spring ...

She who taught us everything ...
How to live and how to sing.
That you can conquer anything .. (with) ...
Chivalry, kindness, courage and the Quest. And by always tryin'- one's very best.
And that sticks and stones could break my bones.
But to love all nature - all of God's tones.
So that names would never actually hurt me ...
And "que-sera, what will be - WILL be."

Queen of Spring ...
In time so short, now you did bring ...
Miracles and happenings.
You who taught us everything ...
Reading, gardening, sewing, cooking, chess.
And how to treat a lady best.
So the bells of life, in joy could ring,
For me to live, in love and sing!
Now a painted lady on the wing ...
I say "Hey, hello again ...
Queen of Spring"

Lyrics by Jayl
Music by Jayl / Sayer / Pepin
From the EP - "RETURN OF THE MOON – Serendipity"

Autumn 1962

EPILOGUE

by Niki Glass

There is always a 'before and after' when a life changing event occurs. I was only 15, still at school, and innocently out with my friends one cold November Friday, for a village centre disco. In fact, I'd been to many of these Friday night discos with my friends throughout the year of 1980.
That was all 'before!'
My life changed in an instant when I was asked to dance by a tall and very handsome young man. I was shy and felt awkward at that age, but I was being guided by an irresistible force of destiny as I was moving through to the 'after'... as I said "yes" to the dance, and then "yes" to the date to Dreamland Cinema the next night. I now had a really lovely cool boyfriend and my life was never to be the same again!

And we are still together through the twists and turns of each amazing decade. I am so incredibly proud of my husband for writing out the story of his childhood in care in the 70s, that led him on his path of destiny - a journey to find me and my Mum, and a place of stability in his heart.
I'm proud of him for his indomitable spirit and tireless determination, and for finding the inner strength to have evoked so many memories and make them into words. I know more than anyone else in this world how challenging this has been for him to put together.
Nevertheless, he has now created a narrative of endurance, survival and love during the gloriously nostalgic 60's and 70's.

"We do have it in us – New spirit has arrived …
The joy and the sorrow – We have a story and it survived" ❤

ABBA – "I Still Have Faith in You"

CREDITS

Pictures and Illustrations: - Many photos in this book are personal pics, taken by the author or those connected with the author. However, some pics have been found on the internet, after Google searches. Every effort has been made to credit these photos, where the info is available. Should anyone see a picture for which they own the copyright, but is not correctly accredited – please get in touch with the author, and the situation will be rectified in forthcoming editions and on social media.

Rock and Roll Music lyrics © Entertainment One U.S. Lp, Kanjian Music

I Still Have Faith In You lyrics © Universal Music Publishing Ab

Giving It All Away lyrics © Universal Music Publishing Group

Life on Mars lyrics © BMG Rights Management, Sony/ATV Music Publishing LLC, Ultra Tunes, Warner Chappell Music, Inc

I Am the Sea lyrics © Spirit Catalog Holdings, S.a.r.l., Fabulous Music Ltd

Broadway lyrics © Nineden Ltd. Songwriters: Mick Jones / Paul Simonon / Joe Strummer

Bell Boy lyrics © Spirit Catalog Holdings, S.a.r.l., Fabulous Music Ltd

Chiming lyrics © Harmony Music

Party photos by Tina Stevens ©

Rear Cover Picture by Peter Bryenton © Brypix

AUTHOR'S NOTE

Special Thanks to Niki, David Meader + Jackie White and Karen Logan @ Spurgeons, for their help and inspiration in the construction of this work. Most of all, thank you to everyone who played a part in my story – whether by intent or design, or completely unintentionally.
Either way, I am eternally grateful to you all. **JCGL**

FURTHER READING & BROWSING

16 Years in Care – *David Meader*
12 Rules For Life - An Anecdote to Chaos – *Dr.Jordan Peterson*
You v The World - The Guide to Never Giving Up – *Bear Grylls*
Faith's Checkbook – *Charles Haddon Spurgeon*
The Screwtape Letters – *C.S. Lewis*
The Holy Bible ✞
Chariots of the Gods – *Erich von Däniken*
Beyond the Magic Pill – *Odille Rault*
On Writing – *Stephen King*
Adventures in Space and Time – *Professor Brian Cox*
The Prophet – *Kahil Gibran*
Manual of the Warrior of Light – *Paulo Coelho*
The Alchemist – *Paulo Coelho*
Dr.Syn on the High Seas – *Russell Thorndike*

JAYL.NET
youtube.com/JAYLTV
youtube.com/@CoachOfLife
HarmonySchool.co.uk
ArsenalGloucester.com
Glaucomarize.org
Spurgeons.org

Dymchurch Wall by Jayl